Digitalization

Conceptually, as well as practically, digitalization is similar to the implementation of a modern computation model – the model may be a centralized setup using a mainframe or it may be extended to an N-tier architecture. Regardless of the specifics of the implementation, however, the conceptual model of data processing remains the same. Digitalization is nothing but a system relying on digital technologies to create, conduct and, potentially, expand a business activity of some sort. Digitalization can be used to create an e-commerce model for a small business or to create a global supply and distribution chain geared toward almost any kind of a business. It could also be used for non-profit purposes, such as on-line education and telemedicine or e-government.

Digitalization: Contexts, Roles, and Outcomes is a contemplation and analysis of the socio-technical system that is known as digitalization. It considers the context of digitalization as well as the ways by which digitalization offers value to the context within which it operates. This book aims to offer readers an entry point to a path of inquiry into the different aspects of digitalization. The goal is to identify main directions for further inquiry, as well as to outline the most obvious obstacles along the way. The book aims to guide readers on their own unique journeys using the basic ideas, principles, and concepts synthesized, developed, and presented in the book. It is beneficial to both practitioners and researchers.

The book covers:

- The functionality of digitalization
- The significance of digitalization
- Identifying the context of digitalization
- Designing a control system
- A cognitive model for the theory of digitalization
- Designing a theory of digitalization

The book helps readers to consider the subject of digitalization in a rigorous and rational way so their own perspectives can emerge stronger and be substantiated and reinforced by building an argument vis-à-vis perspectives and points examined in this book.

Digitalization

Contexts, Roles, and Outcomes

Sergey V. Samoilenko

Routledge
Taylor & Francis Group

NEW YORK AND LONDON

First Edition published 2023
by Routledge
605 Third Avenue, New York, NY 10158

and by Routledge
4 Park Square, Milton Park, Abingdon, Oxon, OX14 4RN

Routledge is an imprint of the Taylor & Francis Group, an informa business

ISBN: 978-1-032-11409-5 (hbk)
ISBN: 978-1-032-30397-0 (pbk)
ISBN: 978-1-003-30490-6 (ebk)

DOI: 10.1201/9781003304906

Typeset in Minion Pro
by KnowledgeWorks Global Ltd.

Contents

About the Author

Sergey V. Samoilenko is a Professor in the Department of CIS/CS at Averett University, Danville, Virginia. He holds his PhD and MS in Information Systems from Virginia Commonwealth University. Sergey's research is focused on the areas of Information Technologies for development, decision support systems, and design of quantitative multi-method methodologies. He is an author of multiple books and book chapters and has published in a variety of journals, as well as in numerous conference proceedings. Sergey can be reached at samoilenko@averett.edu.

Overview

The purpose of this book is to engage a reader in a discussion about some of the issues and aspects relevant to the subject of digitalization. The primary goal is neither to cover, nor to summarize the published research done in this area. Neither the purpose is to delve into the details of various case studies. There will be no references to articles or books – all that is in this text is a, pretty much, a common sense' discussion on the subject.

Instead, the primary intent is to contemplate and analyze the socio-technical system that is known as *digitalization*, to consider the context of digitalization, as well as to consider some of the ways by which digitalization offers its value to the context within which it operates. As a result, we hope this effort may offer a reader an entry to a path of inquiry into variety of the aspects of digitalization, where the goal is to identify main directions for a further inquiry, as well as to outline the most obvious obstacles along the way. Consequently, we hope that the interested reader can continue on her unique journey using the basic ideas, principles, and concepts synthesized, developed, and presented in this book.

We hope that the material presented in this book would be especially beneficial to the practitioners and researchers working in the area of digitalization, where by reading the presented content one can agree or disagree with the points developed by the author. Our reader does not have to agree, or disagree, on the presented points, for the only requirement is to consider the subject of digitalization in more or less a rigorous and rational way, so our reader's own perspective can emerge stronger and be substantiated, or reinforced, by building an argument vis-à-vis perspectives and takes introduced in this book.

In any case, and regardless of "Yeah" or "Nay" on any particular point stated in the text, the reader, as a result of reflecting on the subject, would end up further along in his/her own contemplation and investigation of digitalization. This is simply because that our reader found something to agree or disagree with, and was invited to create her own opinion. For this purpose, we leave the space at the end of each chapter for those who are interested to make their own notes and arguments, and to pose possible research questions related to digitalization as we go along with the chapters of the book.

The text can be approached in two ways. First, a reader could follow a sequence of chapters as arranged within the book. Second, a reader could view the contents as a collection of three interrelated parts. Part 1 focuses on fundamental assumptions and the structure of digitalization. Part 2 deals with functionality of digitalization, its behavior, as well as with constructing a candidate *Theory of Digitalization*. Part 3 considers the intended impact of digitalization and the expected context-specific differences in the impact. Chapter 1 serves as an introductory chapter to all three parts. Next, we provide a brief overview of the topic that each chapter aims to cover.

Chapter 1 is dedicated to the goal of conceptualizing what digitalization is – in this chapter we aim to provide a general well-structured definition of the term and to demonstrate the importance of the precise definition to research and practice.

Chapter 2 deals with the selection of the appropriate lens for investigating digitalization. In this chapter, we present our arguments for why digitalization should be viewed as a *complex system* and why *Complex System Theory* and *Chaos Theory* are good lenses to apply when studying digitalization.

Chapter 3 is concerned with two questions – how to analyze a current state of digitalization and how to plan its future state. The point the chapter makes is that unless we know what "this thing" called digitalization is, we cannot adequately plan for the future – for what "this thing" is going to be and what is it is supposed to do.

Chapter 4 attempts to explicate the fundamental assumption underlying digitalization. This allows for a more disciplined approach to discussing what the essential structural elements of digitalization must be. Intuitively, it is important to know whether the structural components of digitalization are, indeed, the components that *must be* the part of the system.

Chapter 5 builds on developments of the previous chapter and identifies the essential components of a complex system that we refer to as "digitalization". Specifically, the content of the chapter is dedicated to the delineation between a social and a technical components comprising the system.

Chapter 6 extends the considerations of Chapter 5 and investigates the functionality of digitalization. By asking "What is digitalization supposed to do, exactly?", this chapter pinpoints the subprocesses that must be completed within the system in order to deliver the outcome to the context.

Chapter 7 has a main purpose of identifying ways of improving performance of digitalization as of "input-output" system. Specific venues for improvements are identified, and the consequences of the improvements are pointed out.

Chapter 8 considers the impact of digitalization on its internal environment. This chapter looks into directions that digitalization may follow to optimize its internal performance in order to deliver the desired end result to its context.

Chapter 9 is dedicated to the impact of digitalization on its external environment. By considering that the context of digitalization is an open dynamic system, this chapter identifies some of the possible changes that expansion of digitalization may bring to its external environment.

Chapter 10 raises the issue of significance of digitalization. By asking the question "Why is digitalization important?", the chapter points to the context as the obvious reason of being of digitalization. It is noted that the *importance* manifests itself on different levels, and that it is relative to a type of a customer.

Chapter 11 points out that in order to improve the impact of digitalization, the mechanism of the impact needs to be known or, at least, hypothesized. Thus, this chapter considers some of the types of the models that could serve as foundations for *Theory of Digitalization*.

Chapter 12 is concerned with the context of digitalization – the larger system within which digitalization supposed to generate its impact. Two fundamental roles are identified as a result of the analysis – *digital consumers* and *digital activists*.

Chapter 13 considers using digitalization for the purposes of acquiring a digital platform, as well as the benefits that such acquisition provides. The chapter points out the importance of the customers' perspectives on defining the outcome of digitalization.

Chapter 14 builds on the previous chapter and goes a step further by asking "What are the outcomes of using a newly acquired digital platform?" This chapter identifies some important differences between digital consumers and digital activists in terms of the goals they pursue, as well as in terms of their expectations for the outcomes of digitalization.

Chapter 15 aims to outline a scope of digitalization for digital consumers and digital activists. The question of "How deeply digitalization can be embedded within its context?" is asked and some of the scenarios are suggested.

Chapter 16 is directed at identifying outcomes of digitalization. Specifically, the chapter's aim is to develop an idea of what is it, specifically, digitalization can provide to its context – what is the value of using digitalization and where that value comes from?

Chapter 17 investigates the impact of the pressures of the context of digitalization on its structural components – social and technical subsystems. This chapter considers the impact of internal as well as external forces on digitalization, and reflects on how a complex dynamic system may react to those forces.

Chapter 18 is dedicated to the application of digitalization within a non-competitive context of social groups comprised of digital activists. The chapter identifies a possible social stratification as a consequence and a response to using digitalization in such context.

Chapter 19, unlike a previous chapter, places the usage of digitalization within a competitive social context, which brings some additional complexity to considerations of the previous chapter. However, it is still a context that allows for the development and a balanced growth of digitalization.

Chapter 20 is dedicated to considering digitalization being used by adversarial social groups – and the implications that such context brings to the structure and the behavior of digitalization. The analysis of the scenario suggests a set of important implications that must be considered to manage digitalization successfully.

Chapter 21 raises the question of inevitable conflict that is brought about by certain scenarios involving digitalization. The main question of the chapter is "How a conflict environment can be managed?" The chapter demonstrates some of the benefits of using *Chaos Theory* in order to answer the question and propose the solution.

Chapter 22 considers a design of a system capable of managing the conflict environment of digitalization that is brought about by the disturbances in its internal behavior and the changes in structure. The content of the chapter demonstrates that the principles of *Cybernetics* could be used as a guide in proposing a conceptual design of such control system.

Chapter 23 returns to the issue of theory building and constructs a cognitive model for *Theory of Digitalization*. The resultant framework is the model that is flexible and easily extendible to a variety of domains.

Chapter 24 extends the contents of the previous chapter by using the developed cognitive model for the purposes of designing *Theory of Digitalization*. A set of possible research questions and hypotheses are presented to a reader to demonstrate the simplicity and flexibility of the developed theory. This concludes the book.

Introduction

Trouble with Words

A purpose of any language is to enable a process of communication, and this purpose is achieved, fundamentally, by relying on linguistic constructs we call *words*. To that extent a "word" is a made up token that has an assigned meaning and stands for something or expresses something. In that role a word can be viewed as a *sign* – a reference to something empirically accessible (e.g., table, tree), or a word could be perceived as a *symbol* – a pointer to something conceptual yet accessible by proxy (e.g., love, black hole) or transcendental – something accessible only via meta-proxies (e.g., God, Brahman, Good, Evil).

Some words are *terms*. A *term* is a word, or a collection of words, that is *intended to convey a specific meaning in a specific context*. For example, "and" is a word indicating that two things go together – with the meaning "to connect" or "to add". However, in electronics "and" has a specific meaning – the *word* becomes a *term* by acquiring a meaning of *a Boolean operator which gives the value one if and only if all the operands are one, and otherwise has a value of zero* (https://languages.oup.com/google-dictionary-en/). Similarly, *pancreatitis* is a medical term denoting *a condition of inflammation of the pancreas*, and it means, as a *term*, much more to a medical doctor, than, as a *word*, to a lay person on a street. We can say that the meaning of the terms is not universally distributed among the people who use it.

We can see the relationship between "words" and "terms" as a *hierarchy of meanings* – a "word" could be upgraded to a "term" via provision of a specific meaning in a form of a definition, and a "term" can be downgraded to a "word" via wide spread adoption that removes the specific meaning replacing it with a vague idea for what it supposed to denote originally. For example, "freedom of speech" is a well-defined legal term that becomes a string of words with a loose meaning if used in the context of the general population. On the other hand, such common and long used words as "insanity" and "reasonable person" became upgraded to becoming well-defined legal terms with a specific meaning in the field of Law.

But, regardless of the rigor with which words and terms are defined, in order for them to be utilized for the purposes of communication, they must become *common*. This implies that their meaning must be commonly understood, for this is a prerequisite for words and terms becoming a part of a *common language*. Simply put, we have to encode our messages using the same conversion scheme – be it an English language, or ASCII, or Manchester scheme. It is fair to say that the efficiency and effectiveness of the process of communication via a common language is impacted by the precision with which the words and terms comprising the language are defined and, therefore, understood by the users of the language.

Let us turn our attention to a subset of the common language that is represented by *well-defined words* – this places *terms* within that subset. Consequently, within the context of our discussion we use *word* in the sense of a *well-defined syntactic structure with a clearly stated meaning*, where:

- "well-defined" means (based on Merriam-Webster' dictionary – see https://www.merriam-webster.com/dictionary):
  1. *having clearly distinguishable limits, boundaries, or features*, or,
  2. *clearly stated or described*
- "meaning" is *the thing one intends to convey especially by language* (https://www.merriam-webster.com/dictionary/meaning).

In short, in our discussion we are dealing with those *words* that are *terms*.

One of the goals we pursue in this text is very simple – we want to demonstrate to our reader some of the aspects of a potential problem associated with a utilization of poorly defined words with an ambiguous meaning in a common language. Specifically, we would like to call an attention to *hype words* – those linguistic constructs that came to existence and became popular within a specific subset of a society, and then became "released into the wild" for a consumption by the general public. The word of interest to us is *digitalization*, and we are aiming to discuss with our reader a hidden complexity behind the concept that underlies it.

It all starts with *digitization*, which is *the process of using digital information technologies to convert analog data into its digital counterpart*. If Paul scanned his drawing, then he used digitization in the process. And if we use digitization to improve the existing state of affairs in business and to change, or create new, business models and streams of revenue, then we get *digitalization*. If Scott, how is a hairdresser, uses his phone to schedule his appointments (instead of serving only walk-ins) and to automatically reorder his barbershop supplies from the vendor (instead of doing so in person), then Scott used digitalization to do so. And if we use digitization to change/transform major (or all) aspects of a business, then we get *digital transformation. Instagram* story is illustrative of digital transformation that did miracles for Instagram, bud did not bode too well for Kodak. Mostly, delineating lines are blurry – go figure where "major change" ends and "transformation" begins.

For the purposes of this study we adopt the following definition (provided by Gartner Group – see: https://www.gartner.com/en/information-technology/glossary)

> *Digitalization is the use of digital technologies to change a business model and provide new revenue and value-producing opportunities; it is the process of moving to a digital business.*

Given this definition, we consider *platformization* to be a subset of *digitalization*, because a former requires the latter, while the latter offers opportunities beyond the former. We use the following definition of a *platform* (similarly, provided by Gartner Group):

> *A platform is a product that serves or enables other products or services.*

And we define (our own definition due to the absence of the established one) *digital platformization* as:

> *A process of development and utilization of a digital interface – of a digital product that serves or enables other products or services.*

And, from this point on, we refer to the subject of our interest as *digitalization.*

But, let us pause for a moment and ask the following question: *Why not to call digitalization and platformization using simpler terms – digital interface* and *digital interface' development?* The answer is simple – by acquiring a fancier label the subject also acquires the air of sophistication otherwise not perceived by those who are not "in the know". Simply put, *the Cloud* sounds cooler and is easier to sell than *N-tier distributed architecture.* This substitution, of course, makes a perfect business sense, because a person aiming to "elucidate the perilous consequences of perfunctory implementation of digitalization" commands a greater level of attention and resources from her "not in the know" colleagues, then a person speaking in a plain language would. Be it academia or business, the size, the magnitude, and the extent of the allocated resources matters in the Darwinian fight for survival of the fittest and the most funded. One cannot escape dealing with triple constrain of scope, cost, and time.

We must note that the current work is not definition-dependent. This is because, for all intents and purposes, all available definitions of *digitalization* or *platformization* (as well as definitions of majority of IS-related concepts) are so severely lacking, that they all proudly wear large targets on their backs to invite a lethal dose of criticism. A lot of it is too general, and a lot of what is too general is by design, so a sale could be made or a paper could be published.

Instead, our work is suggestive in spirit – we aim to advocate for precision and specificity in terms and definitions used in the field of Information Systems. Such terms as "the Cloud", "cybersecurity", "ICT4D", "business intelligence", and so on, do sound grand to lay people and they do add pizzazz to sale pitches, but they do not add to the progress of the field, and they do not help telling a true story of what is it that the field of Information Systems is trying to accomplish. But, it is only if we know what is it that we are trying to do, with what resources, and for what purpose, only then we can actually assess the current state of the efforts and to adequately plan for the desired future. And, as an added benefit, will be able to explain to others outside of the field, clearly and specifically, what is it we are trying to do, which is not a bad idea also.

1

Conceptualizing and Defining Digitalization

While it is a use of a common language or some sort of communication that makes interactions productive, that allows individual people to aggregate and form societies, there is also something else that is needed – a shared culture. Even in a very diverse and multicultural society, there must be a common understanding of the nature of *everyday reality* among its members – a *weltanschauung* that supports the shared culture and allows the society to function.

It is worth noting the importance of the concept of "everyday reality" – it is *a legally, ethically, formally, and informally bound subset of the social, physical, and cultural world that is shared by the individuals living in a given society*. Meaning, an atheist, a Muslim, a Christian, a Jew, and a Buddhist may all have their own views on the nature of the "big R" *Reality* – each one of them would have their own *big weltanschauung,* which may be quite incompatible or outright irreconcilable with that of their counterparts. However, as long as they share a common *little weltanschauung* pertaining to *everyday reality within a given context,* they can co-exist in the same society quite comfortably and to their mutual benefit. Regardless of whether you subscribe to modernist or postmodernist philosophical principles, you still have to pay your taxes, and over-the-board Satanists pay for their groceries just as well-behaving Christians do.

Leaving out the inevitable uniform acceptance of the common physical laws by the members of a society (e.g., if you drop your sandwich it falls due to the force of gravity), the individuals must agree on *little weltanschauung,* and this agreement means accepting a shared meaning of the words that describe it. This agreement is forged via the process of *acculturation* – by utilizing its formal and informal components. Formally, the

DOI: 10.1201/9781003304906-1

acculturation takes place when an individual participates in formal social transactions *vis-a-vis* other members of the society. For example, if Mary attended Best University and was taught a definition of "computer network", which she then used in conversations with her neighbor, then Mary acquired a shared meaning of the term via the process of *formal acculturation*, and then she re-enforced that meaning via the process of *informal acculturation*.

On the other hand, if Bob, who knows nothing about different types of computer architecture, brings his laptop to his friend and is told that he cannot print any longer because he needs to update his device driver, then Bob just learned that a device driver is an "important thing that allows a laptop to print", and he acquired this shared meaning via the process of informal acculturation. If, after this encounter, Bob submits his request to update a device driver to the Help Desk at his work, and his request is understood by the representative, then Bob re-enforced and validated the meaning of "device driver" via the process of formal acculturation.

Those are different venues, and we would like them to work in unison and synergy by providing a congruency between the meanings they supply. Most of the times they do – when a girl starts attending her school, she is taught to value her education by her teacher in a classroom (e.g., formal acculturation), but she is also told to value her education by her parents at home (e.g., informal acculturation). However, sometimes they do not play well together – when a young man is told that alcohol is poison by his doctor (e.g., formal acculturation), but is persuaded by his friends that alcohol is fun (e.g., informal acculturation), then what we have is a conflict to deal with.

As an interlude, let us ask a question: What does "digitalization" mean and what does this term stand for? At this point, there is no shared meaning of digitalization that can be reliably acquired through either formal or informal processes of acculturation. We use the clause "reliably" to indicate not the shortage of the practitioners and academics willing to define the term and explain it to willing bystanders, but a lack of consistency in the assigned meaning to the term.

However, an agreement, we must have…. And once the agreement regarding everyday reality is achieved, then even some *big weltanschauung*-related concepts could be incorporated successfully into an understanding of *little weltanschauung* – this allows for such phrases as "Don't do it – there will be hell to pay!", "His new business is in limbo", "This tastes like heaven!" to be understood in the same way by an atheist, a Muslim, a Christian, a Jew, or a Buddhist.

At this point, we can summarize the stated above content as the following assertion (A#):

A1: One of the prerequisites for a functioning society is a common understanding by its members of the meaning of the words that describe:

1. The society in general, and
2. The everyday reality of living in that society in particular.

A viable society is a dynamic and open system, and a viable dynamic system transitions through its states – let us say, its past, its present, and its future. This allows us to put forward the second assertion:

A2: A common understanding of the meaning of words allows a functioning society to analyze its past, to assess its present, and to plan for its future.

Just consider a phrase "The day was young and life was beautiful and Bob was gay, but when the clouds rolled in he was no more". There are ways to understand this sentence…

This implies that the viability of a society is dependent, at least in part, on a common understanding and shared interpretation of the meaning of the words in the vocabulary used by the members of the society. For example, if we are to inquire into changes regarding the state of infrastructure of Information and Communication Technology (ICT) in the US, and if we are to plan for its future state, then we must, clearly, define what "ICT infrastructure" is and how we are going to represent it and how we are going to measure it.

Taking this into consideration, it is clear, prior to even reading, that a hypothetical article titled "Assessing State of Cybersecurity: Past, Present, and Future" will contain, highly likely, a lot of hype words and not a lot of substance. And this is not a reason for antagonism toward the author who wants to publish his paper or the subject – it is that the breadth of the undertaking makes a meaningful assessment impossible. But, if a reader attends to the content of the article, then it is the fault of the reader because it is he who gives the authority to the writer and the subject.

After all, when one sees a paper titled "Assessing State of Health…" or "Assessing Quality of Movies…", one does not expect a serious treatment of the topic. However, it is, probably, fair to say that a conference titled "Assessing State of Digitalization: Past, Present, and Future" would attract a large share of participants who are in awe and bewilderment of the topic. The *cool* factor is hard to beat.

In this work, we are primarily concerned with the issues facing us in assessing its present and planning its future, specifically, in the context that impacts, and is impacted by, digitalization. Thus, we put forward yet another assertion:

> A3: A lack of a common understanding of the meaning of words precludes a functioning society from adequately assessing its present state and planning for its future.

On its own, this is not big of a problem, for it is reasonable to suggest that in order to facilitate a common understanding of a word or a phrase, all we need to do is to provide a common definition.

This, a seemingly simple task, is not easy to accomplish – this is why we have so many terms that lack a common definition at the inter- as well as intra-societal level. Furthermore, the same situation with a lack of a common definition is observable even at a more restrictive sub-cultural level characterized by the same field of inquiry or industry – see Table 1.1.

While there could be many reasons for why certain terms (e.g., happy life, successful career, etc.) and words are not defined or poorly defined or have multiple definitions (see Table 1.2), there is only one consequent – they lead to a lack of a common understanding of the meaning of what is

TABLE 1.1

Examples of Imprecise Meanings

Specific Field	Term or Statement	Precise Meaning?
Information Technology	Big Data, Business Intelligence	No
Business	Status Code, Business Value	No
Law	Probable Cause, Insanity, Reasonable Person	No

TABLE 1.2

Examples of Imprecise Definitions

Term or Statement	Definition?
Fair Business Practices, Social Justice, Green Energy, Good Government	No
Happy Life, Successful Career, Good Person, Customer, Value	No
Fresh Produce, Healthy Meal	Ambiguous
Attack, Authorization	Multiple

being said. Interestingly, the reasons for the misunderstanding are *not* due to the inevitable subjectivity of the interpretation by an individual.

This is because if we are relying on the assumption of the acceptance of *little weltanschauung* by the members of a society, then we must leave the reason of subjectivity of interpretation outside of our consideration. For example, whatever the subjective takes and interpretations of individual stakeholders could be regarding the term "case dismissed", at the end of the day, being in a courtroom, they must be set aside. The reason is simple – in order to remain within the society and its corresponding system of values, all of the involved parties must adopt a commonly accepted within *little weltanschauung* meaning of the term "case dismissed". If this is so, then it implies leaving a subjectivity of interpretation out of our explanatory equation. Let us consider two possible reasons.

The first reason is the comfort and convenience that could be found in using proverbial "umbrella terms". Primarily, this is due to the ambiguity regarding the descriptive attributes of the terms and corresponding vagueness of applicable assessment criteria. Such terms as "Help Desk", "Customer Support", "Health Care Facility", or "Student Success Center" remain terribly attractive and widely used exactly for such reasons. Let us consider a counterexample in the form of a standardized test preparation center – such enterprise provides a well-defined and precise service of improving the test scores of test-takers. Test preparation center clearly defines what the goal is, and what the criterion of success is – and it does so consistently and for each and every customer. This is not a level of precision we used to get from peddlers of cloud, digitalization, and cybersecurity solutions.

Another possible reason, however, lies in the difficulty of translating preferred by humans' Platonic concepts into their Aristotelian counterparts favored by mechanistic structures of definitions. In this case, such terms as "Secure System", "User-Friendly Environment", and so on could serve as good candidate examples. Customers want user-friendly applications, reliable storage, and secure devices, just as they want to be healthy and happy and live a good life and have a good job. Specifics, however, are rarely mentioned, and the fact that there is no free lunch and there is a price to pay for each promised benefit is almost always left untold.

Under the circumstance of having no exact definition or an agreement on the meaning of a term depicting an important concept or an attribute, any society faces the trouble of assessing its current state *vis-à-vis* that concept or attribute. Let us say, we are interested in having a "productive" society that is comprised of "good productive people" – in the absence of the common definition of what "productive" means and its acceptance within *little weltanschauung* of that society no adequate assessment of how the society is doing in this regard is possible. And while a society could resort to proxies and select to measure intelligence via standardized tests and academic success of students via their GPA, the limitations of such recourse are many.

However, let us recap what is said to be known about digitalization at this point in time. And, again, we would like to remind our reader that what is "known" at this point amounts to, pretty much, the same statement as "exercise is good for you". And this is without specifying who "you" are, what "you" do, where to exercise, doing what, specifically, and how often and for how long. All that while completely ignoring your social obligation and peculiarities of your socio-technical context and the ecology of your environment. But, let us consider what is known, at this point, about digitalization and about how digitalization works.

First, there is pretty much a consensus that digitalization works on different levels. For example, it can function within a stratum of:

- *Society*, where digitalization could allow for changes in socio-economic structures and arrangements. This is done by elimination and creation of jobs and job types, and the introduction of new (and elimination of old) decision-making structures. E-government initiatives offer an illustrative example of digitalization functioning at the level of society.
- *Industry*, where digitalization is capable of re-shuffling the existing hierarchies, eliminating or restructuring old, and creating new value nets and value chains. Primary tools of change are new digital interfaces and information channels that allow for disposing the less effective and efficient ones. Extranets and digitalized supply chains are examples of digitalization working at the level of the industry, or even of cross-industries.
- *Organization*, where digitalization enables the offering of new products/services in novel ways while eliminating the less effective and efficient practices. Such initiatives as *Business Process Re-engineering* and the introduction of *Enterprise Systems* are good examples of digitalization operating at the level of a firm.

- *Process,* where digitalization is responsible for automating the previously "analog" sub-processes and task via the adaptation of new digital tools and technologies. A prime example of such impact is a successful *Business Process Automation* initiative that results in the improvements in the process effectiveness, efficiency, and safety.

Second, there is also an agreement regarding how digitalization delivers its "goodies", regardless of the level of the impact. Namely, digitalization makes its host:

- *More internally efficient,* via streamlining and benchmarking business processes relevant to the implementation of the business model of the firm. However, even the supporting processes could benefit from a computer-based increase in internal effectiveness and efficiency (e.g., IT department, HR, and so on).
- *More externally aware,* via opening up new business opportunities by means of easier interactions with the other players on the market, acquiring new customers, dismissing redundant or no longer needed intermediaries. Finally, this is a path to an opportunity via the provision of new services to the context that wants them (e.g., selling digital versions of high-fashion items).
- *More disruptive to its context,* where a host of digitalization is capable of discontinuing some old and established services while, suddenly, offering the new ones in its old and new contexts. This is similar to the concept of "general computer", where such devices could solve a whole host of problems, but only if they lent themselves to be addressed via computation-based methods, and if there are resources that could translate the problems into suitable formulations.

Additionally, there is no disagreement that digitalization could be used to improve different types of business processes – be it *downstream* activities of the type "shipping products to distributors" or *upstream* ones of the type "ordering and receiving parts from the vendor". And, overall, there is a view that digitalization can positively contribute to sustainable development by impacting its main components – economy, society, and environment. The avenues of the impact are many, but commonly mentioned ones are those shared with *globalization* – via increased transparency and accountability of the relevant business processes and associated transactions.

There are multiple instances of repackaging the old initiatives using a shinier wrap of digitalization. For example, it is often noted that digitalization can be of great help in the domain of public services, but, e-government initiatives are old news by now. The same goes for presenting a perspective on digitalization as a new tool of organizational learning, while never mentioning knowledge management initiatives that have been around for many decades.

However, there is also a body of a "received" knowledge in terms of the accumulated general IT-related wisdom, according to which the *implementation of digitalization is not guaranteed to bring positive results* to the host and its ecosystem. This *digitalization paradox* reflecting a failure to capture value from digitalization initiatives might be the result of the impact of such reasons as integration failure due to the complexity of the technological system, lack of investments in complementary areas, and neglect for the social component of digitalization in the form of a failure to develop human skills, competencies, and capabilities.

On the negative side of things, there is a price to pay, for digitalization offers new opportunities for such unlawful activities as digital fraud, and offers new paths of escapism in the form of augmented and virtual reality. At the work – and marketplace, digitalization's reliance on computer technology contributes to elevating few, while dismissing many a worker, thus contributing to the increased inequality that is easily observed in general, but especially so in the developed world. Evidence at the firm level is abundant to suggest that in order for digitalization to succeed, some organizational changes are in order, and those changes *may* create some new jobs, but they will, at the very least, introduce IT-related knowledge and skills' biases into the wage distribution. The resultant divergence of the economic outcomes brought about by digitalization does not only exist at the level of individual workers, but also at the level of the firms and metropolitan areas – all the way to manifest itself in the form of country-level socioeconomic and technological disparities.

This little summary is similar to a set of answers to the question "Why should I exercise?" There are pluses, there are minuses, and no outright guarantees, and no tailored instructions. Instead, the reasons for why one should, based on the points mentioned above, are intuitive. Namely, you should exercise because:

1. Your body will become more efficient
2. You will be more aware of your environment

3. You will be able to adopt to the changes around you better than those who don't exercise.

However, there are reasons why a good advice may not be taken by a party to which it is extended. Some of them are:

I am not sure I need it – I am fine as I am

I am not sure I can do it – I wish I could, but I don't have time/money/ energy/etc.

I am not sure I trust you because I don't know what it is – I wish I could trust you, but you don't have a 100% record of success

I am not sure I trust you because I don't understand the reason for why I need it – why would I want to do something about my future state if I don't feel pressed to do anything about my current state

And so on…

So, more clarity on the subject of digitalization is needed – what it is, how it works, and when to have one and when to say "No, thank you!"

Keeping this in mind our subject, and in order to start our inquiry, we are warranted to pose the following two questions:

1. *What is digitalization, structurally?*
   The purpose of this question is simple – is to state, clearly, what *digitalization*, as a system, consists of. The following sub-questions would have to be posed and answered:
   - What are the sub-systems or sub-parts or components of digitalization?
   - What do the components do – what is the function of each component?
   - What are the relationships between the components?
2. *What is digitalization, functionally?*
   The purpose of answering the second question is also straightforward – it is to state, unambiguously, what the system is intended to do. Here, we need to explain the output that the system, digitalization, is supposed to produce. The following sub-questions would have to be posed and answered:
   - What are the main outputs of digitalization?
   - What are the main processes that allow for producing the outputs?
   - What are the components and their relationships that support each process?

TABLE 1.3

Example of Disambiguation of a Term

Cloud Computing	Disambiguation
What is it, structurally?	An instance of N-tier distributed computing architecture
What are the components?	Clients, servers, transmission media, network devices
What do the components do?	Client – allows the user to generate requests for resources
	Server – listens for requests and sends out requested resources
	Media – allows for communicating signals representing encoded resources
	Network devices – enable routing and interconnection
What are the relationships between the components?	Client→ Server→ Client interaction
	Client→ transmission media→ network device→ Server
What is it, functionally?	A system allowing for decentralized data processing
What are the main outputs?	Data delivered to clients, data stored/processed on servers
What are the main processes?	Generation of a request
	Generation of a response
	Routing/addressing decision
What are the components and their relationships that support each process?	Clients: generate requests and receive requested resources
	Servers: generate responses and send out requested resources
	Routers: make routing/addressing decisions
	Transmission media: enables propagation of signals

By answering these questions, we should be able to acquire some sort of a solid ground to construct more complex questions. For illustrative purposes, let us consider how this structure could be applied to disambiguate the term "Cloud Computing" – presented in Table 1.3.

It is easy to see, that if such structure is followed, then a "hierarchical disambiguation" could easily take place, where the next level of disambiguation could describe what "client" is, and the level after what "hardware" is, and so on. It would be interesting to observe if investigators writing about user satisfaction, technology acceptance, and system security could follow such a structure to present their findings.

One may say that it is often not done because of the complexity of the subject, where information technology and information systems are too complex to define precisely. However, this cannot be a true reason – after all, we can refer to architecture and medicine as reference disciplines that deal with complex issues and subjects, and they don't shy away from being specific. When you get a pain reliever you know what it is made of and what it is supposed to do – the medicine does not promise you to improve your health, and while an architect may create a design of a "three-bedroom house", she will never say that it is a design of a "happy home". Contrary to that, we are "offered secure and reliable cloud storage", "unlimited data", and "lightning-fast connections".

A research-related note: it seems only reasonable to expect that any academic paper that deals with the subject of digitalization should clearly state in its introduction what digitalization is, structurally, and what digitalization supposed to do within a given context.

However, any analysis-based decomposition of such a complex thing as digitalization is based on the perspective selected by the one who is doing the decomposition. The purpose of the next chapter is to suggest to our reader a viable perspective from which digitalization can be inquired into.

READER NOTES

Main points of agreement	
Supporting arguments (why agree?)	
Main points of disagreement	
Supporting arguments (why disagree?)	
Illustrative scenarios	
Possible research problem	
Possible research questions	

2

Conceptualizing Digitalization – What Is a Good Lens to Use?

The question "How to select an appropriate perspective?" is an important one because it impacts the process of a construction of a model to support an inquiry into the subject of our interest – digitalization. After all, models are perspective-specific. Let us consider a simple example of digitalization, as follows:

> A popular local bakery, known for its cookies, makes a decision to start selling its baked goods on-line. In order to do so, digitalization of the business must be undertaken – potential customers must be able to learn about the shop, browse its inventory, and purchase the goods on-line. Additionally, customers, as well as all and any interested parties, may watch videos of cookies being made, and interact, via social networks, with the chief cookie baker.

Conceptually, as well as practically, it is easy to extend this scenario and to creating a global supply and distribution chain geared toward almost any kind of a business. Or, conversely, we could use digitalization for non-profit purposes, such as on-line education and telemedicine or e-government. After all, digitalization is nothing else but a system relying on digital technologies to create, to conduct and, potentially, to expand a business activity of some sort. This is similar to the implementation of a modern model of computation – you can have a centralized set up using a mainframe, or you could extend it to N-tier architecture. But, regardless of the specifics of the implementation, the conceptual model of data processing remains the same.

DOI: 10.1201/9781003304906-2

Let us consider possible perspectives from which we could look at the scenario of *bakery digitalization*, where we could view it as a:

1. *Machine* – a technological artefact comprised of IT components
2. *Information system* comprised of IT, data, users, and policies/procedures
3. *Social system* comprised of owners and customers
4. *Social network* comprised of communication channels and nodes
5. *Political power system* comprised of power-based interactions and conflicts
6. *Social system of oppression* comprised of oppressors and oppressed members
7. *Economic system* geared towards production of revenue that is comprised of labor, investment, and productivity gains
8. and so on, for there is an endless selection of perspectives to choose from.

Clearly, all the perspectives are observer-relevant and could be valid and useful depending on a correctly selected context, and they are all could be perfectly applicable depending on the goal of the study. What is problematic, however, is the scenario when multiple meta-perspectives are mixed and matched at will of the investigator. For example, if we view Facebook as a social system, then questions of technological security of communication channels and data storage simply do not lend themselves to be inquired into within the same study. If we view Walmart as a revenue-generating system, then it is out of place to consider it being a social network. Simply put, if Albert has a broken leg and needs a new prescription for his glasses, then Albert would go to different doctors that apply coherent and mutually non-contradictory, but still different models of a human body.

A research note: it seems only reasonable to expect that an investigator writing about digitalization not only defines its structure and function, but also explicitly states the chosen digitalization weltanschauung – the world-view for the selected instance of digitalization.

But, regardless of the context, in order to look at the available to us options we ask *what is a suitable meta-perspective on digitalization given its endemic characteristics?* And this is an important question to answer, for it would allow us to differentiate between necessary characteristics of digitalization and the manifestations, or reflections, or symptoms of those characteristics. For example, a technological system comprised of

IT components may manifest itself as a social network, or as a source of a revenue, or as a source of user satisfaction, But, those manifestations are projections and are secondary to the primacy of the technological system that underlies their existence and generates them. In other words, there is *digitalization as a virtual machine*, and there is *digitalization as an infrastructure that enables the virtual machine.*

Similarly, a human being could be viewed as a member of a society, as an athlete, as a worker, as a family member, and so on. But, what should we view a human being as? What would be an appropriate meta-perspective? Well, an atheist perspective would differ from a perspective of theist, and the perspective of Western philosophy would paint a different picture than a perspective of a traditional Eastern philosophy would. And in the same way an organic view will generate a different perspective on a subject of interest than a mechanistic view would. Some sort of a higher common ground, a unifying meta-perspective, must be in place to weave a nomological network that furthers our state of knowledge about the subject or phenomenon of interest.

Let us also consider some of the most obvious alternatives in terms of the perspectives on digitalization that are available to us.

- First, we can view digitalization through a mechanistic lens, but such perspective abstracts away non-linearity of the relationships and simplifies the environment too much. A utilization of a photo booth is an example of digitalization viewed and implemented via mechanistic perspective.
- Or, we can view digitalization as a social network, but such take would leave us de-emphasizing a technical component of the subject. The unfortunate corollary is that such perspective may lead us to equating, in principle, an IT-based social network with a group of face-to-face participants.
- We can also view digitalization from an organic perspective – this is, probably, a better lens to use if we want to view digitalization as an organism and to consider the presence of non-linearity of interactions and emergent properties. However, we should keep in mind that digitalization is something that people build, and not give birth to. Also, the resultant model would, inevitably, end up being too complex for us to deal with (as the field of medicine demonstrates).
- As well as a variety of other options – we can view digitalization as a political power system, a system of social domination, an economic system, and so on.

Taking our options into realistic consideration, we suggest that digitalization can be perceived as a *complex system (CS)* that can be successfully viewed through the lens of *Complex Systems Theory* (CST). As a result, we state that suggestion in the form of the proposition supporting our inquiry:

> Digitalization is a socio-technical artefact that can be viewed as a Complex System and investigated using a lens of Complex Systems Theory.

In this context, the term *complexity* of a system refers to *the extent of the difficulty (e.g., complex in the sense of not simple) in describing the structure and behavior and possible states of the system that is changing as a response to the environmental disturbances.* Given such characterization, it is easy to see that a human being is a good candidate to be viewed as a complex system, while a computer might not be. It is fair to say that complex systems are everywhere, and it is not surprising that many scientific disciplines study the subject of complexity – this is, perhaps, why there is no single unified definition of the term available.

It is important to note that this Complex Systems' perspective does not dictate what the components of a system must be – CST does not indicate that components must be logical, or that the components must be physical. Instead, CST suggests that whatever fits the bill of a complex system could be viewed as a collection of components. So, if we take a university as an example of a complex system, then we can say that it is comprised of many departments (a logical construct), and those departments are comprised of people (a physical construct), and every physical person is a complex system as well.

As in the case of the term *complexity*, we don't have a common definition of what *Theory of Complexity* is. But, despite the absence of a *unified theory* of complexity, we have at our disposal acknowledged and *unified traits* that are common to all theories and perspectives and studies of complexity – namely, they all deal with *dynamic adaptive systems comprised of multiple interrelated components.* Let us now take a closer look at those unified traits and common characteristics.

COMPLEX SYSTEMS THEORY AND CHAOS THEORY

Within the domain of CST, the term *system* refers to any entity that consists of multiple components and can be viewed from a dual perspective, as a single thing, or as a collection of constituting it parts. Absence of universally accepted definition of complexity makes a CS hard to define, but easy to recognize, for such systems exhibit a common set of basic characteristics. The first characteristic refers to the number of elements comprising it, where a CS is a system that made up of a large number of interacting heterogeneous components. The interactions between the elements of a CS are associated with the presence of a feedback mechanism, and this causes behavior of the system to be hard to predict due to *non-linearity* of the feedback-controlled type of a behavior.

A large number of components interacting in a non-linear fashion give rise to the second characteristic of CS, that of *emergent properties*, which refers to the appearance of independently observable and empirically verifiable patterns of the collective behavior of the system. A system is *dynamic* if its state or behavior changes with time. Parts of a computer are not dynamic in terms of their relative states – a RAM stick cannot decide to turn itself into cache memory to help out, but a construction crew is dynamic in this regard, and this is why a carpenter, while waiting for his resources to arrive, can volunteer (via assuming a different role) to help his co-worker who is a mason. A project team that relies on any of the Agile methodologies is a dynamic non-linear system, where every member of the team could play multiple roles depending on the needs and the state of the project, and where the information channels (e.g., relationships) between the members of the team change based on the roles the members perform.

The systems that we are interested in are *deterministic* in terms of the cause and effect. Thus, if we define a complex dynamic system through a set of equations, then the variables would relate to each other in a non-probabilistic way, i.e., only in terms of "0" or "1". There is an important distinction between *determinism* of a system and its *predictability*. While earlier states in a deterministic system do *determine* later ones, our knowledge of earlier states does not necessarily allow us to *predict* later states of the system. For example, if we administer a deadly poison to a person, then we know, deterministically, that it will result in death of the person who received the poison. However, we may not be able to predict when, exactly, it is going to happens. In a similar fashion we can say that Freshman Joe will fail his Math class or classes if he does not study – in this case the relationship "*If* study, *then* pass" is deterministic. However, we cannot predict when Joe will fail his class – in the beginning, in the middle, or by the end of a semester. As well as we cannot say whether it is going to happen at the level of Math101, Math109, or Math121. But, the causality in the form of "*If* not study, *then* fail" is there.

Because the provided above characterizations are quite general, we would expect a great variability among the non-linear dynamic systems, along with the variability of the patterns of behavior that they exhibit. Subject of a study of *Chaos Theory* (CT) is a large class of complex non-linear dynamic systems capable of exhibiting chaotic pattern of behavior. Intuitively, we don't expect to apply this theory to all systems that *appear to be of the same type*. For example, let us consider a socio-technical system that is stressed by its competitive environment – while we may expect a business firm to behave chaotically under stress of its competitors, we do not, really, expect military units to behave in the same way when in action. Also, intuitively, we expect that the occurrence of the chaotic behavior is to be partially dependent on the presence of discretionary and unstable information channels of communication between the components comprising a complex system.

We define CT as a *qualitative study of unstable aperiodic behavior in deterministic non-linear dynamic systems*. It is a *qualitative* study because rates of change are expressed in terms of non-linear equations, and there exist no general formula for arriving at solutions for successive points in time. CT is the study of *unstable behavior* because a non-linear dynamic system responds to even small perturbations in significant ways where, for example, chaotic systems are *hypersensitive* to initial conditions. Finally, the behavior is *aperiodic* because of the nature of non-linear interactions of the system's variables. I am sure we all have witnessed how a behavior of a person, or a group of people, can become unstable – in the sense of the behavior gradually becoming unpredictable. And what sets one group of people off is not the same thing or event that triggers the unstable behavior in another group.

Viewing a complex non-linear dynamic system through the lens of CT allows us to perceive such system as consisting of two components. The first component is a unique set of *initial conditions*. The second component is a set of formulae representing the *dynamic* part of the system, which is a non-unique *rule* defining the *intended trajectory* of the system's states. And it is the difference in initial conditions that forces a unique evolutionary path of a system through the set of its states. It happens because inevitable small errors made in specifying the initial state of a system grow and eventually dominate the future behavior of the system, causing the actual path to deviate farther and farther from the defined by the *rule* trajectory. Thus, it is not surprising that two businesses following exactly the same path to the intended prosperity may diverge in regard to the final result, and diverge greatly. A good example is a difference in a relative performance of franchise operations, such as McDonalds fast food restaurants.

This is a point where a relative complexity, or a *dimension* designating the number of variables required to describe the system at a given state, plays an important role. The feedback mechanisms of the CS with the dimension of three or more prevent the errors from growing to infinity. Instead, a CS can go through extremely complicated behavior. When mapped on the *phase space*, an abstract geometrical space representing states of the system in time, behavior of a CS could exhibit three different patterns. Namely, it may tend to the *state of equilibrium*, it may tend to *repetitive periodic behavior*, or it may behave *chaotically*.

Such behaviors are observable in the business environment, where a firm could be in a steady-state of functioning – this is common in the case of a relatively static business environment (e.g., selling landscaping tools to homeowners in the areas with little deviation in weather conditions). A case of a repetitive periodic behavior is observable in the firms operating in the markets impacted by seasonality (e.g., fashion retail business), where there is an observable "season/off season" type of a pattern (e.g., Black Friday & Christmas vs. the rest of the year). Finally, businesses often display a chaotic type of a behavior when undergoing internal restructuring associated with mergers and acquisitions, bankruptcies, and changes in the target markets.

Behavior of a system can be represented in terms of an *attractor*, which is a set of points in the phase space that defines its steady state motion. Every attractor has a *basin of attraction*, or a set of points in the space of system variables that evolve to a particular attractor. Aperiodically fluctuating systems said to have a *strange* attractor. Strange attractors are *chaotic* when the trajectories in the phase space, from two points very close on the attractor, diverge exponentially due to the system's sensitive dependence on initial conditions and small perturbations in control parameters. The second important insight provided by CT is that while evolutionary path of chaotic system is not predictable, the *pattern of the path* could be predicted.

Another insight provided by CT is that a system might have multiple attractors associated with multiple patterns of behavior. A CS can transition from a semi-stable to a chaotic state. This happens when a value of key parameter of a system increases and exceeds a threshold value, forcing a single outcome basin to expand into two distinct causal fields. This process of doubling of a number of basins, or *bifurcation*, can safely continue up to the point of a system having eight basins of attraction. However, the next bifurcation marks the *onset of chaos*.

DIGITALIZATION, CST, AND CT

To argue the point that digitalization could be viewed through the lenses of CST and CT, we follow a systematic approach of eligibility assessment presented in Table 2.1.

Let us make another note regarding a criterion of determinism and, specifically, as it relates to predictability. Determinism implies causality, but it does not mean that *a state of a causal system is always predictable* – determinism does not equate with predictability. Meaning, we may relate, deterministically, an additional position of software engineer and the expected increase in the level of software production. However, we cannot predict whether the actual hiring of a software engineer shall, indeed, result in the intended outcome. Simply put, more gas in the tank of a car implies longer distance the car can travel, but there is no guarantee – we

TABLE 2.1

Digitalization as a Complex System

Criterion	Assessment of Eligibility
Complexity	Because it takes more than three variables to describe at a given state, it qualifies as CS in terms of the number of components.
Non-Linearity	Digitalization is a socio-technical system, and socio-technical systems contain non-linear relationships.
Emergent Properties	There is a variety of ways by which emergent properties can manifest themselves in any IS: as a mosaic e-mail correspondence, as a new network bottleneck, or as a social/political power relationship.
Dynamic	Emergent properties change with time, suggesting the dynamic nature of digitalization.
Deterministic	Determinism refers to the defined relationship between variables in the system. Digitalization is a system constructed on the basis of causal relationships: we "know" that the increased bandwidth must contribute to the throughput and we "know" that improved virus protection must contribute to the security of the system. All examples may exhibit a different degree of cause and effect, but that the cause and effect relationships exist between them is certain and not "probable".

cannot predict – that the car with a full tank is going to travel the distance (e.g., because of the flat tire, transmission failure, or illness of the driver). The simplest example of such *deterministic yet unpredictable* situation is any biological life form – we can say, with certainty, that the life form will die if it was born – in this sense the birth determines, with certainty, the death. However, we cannot be so certain when making a statement regarding the time frame between the two states of a biological system.

Overall, it seems reasonable to qualify digitalization as a complex non-linear dynamic system. Consequently, we are justified in stating that *digitalization is a complex system that is:*

- *Comprised of multiple components*
- *Characterized by non-linear interactions between the components*
- *Exhibits a purposeful observable behavior*
- *Open to its environment*
- *Exists in a particular state*
- *Capable of changing its state (e.g., behavior and structure) in response to its environment*

And if digitalization qualifies as complex system, then the structure, function, and behavior of digitalization can be inquired into through the lens of CT.

The benefit is obvious – by using CST we can view digitalization as a technological system, as a social system, as an economic system, or as a network. All the while relying on the same meta-perspective. Let us take a look and briefly examine whether digitalization qualifies as a complex system – we will do so by examining attributes of complex systems *vis-à-vis* attributes of digitalization. A more detailed assessment is presented later in the chapter.

DIGITALIZATION IS A COMPLEX SYSTEM

The first attribute is a *complexity of structure* – complex systems are comprised of multiple components and digitalization, as it is known to us today, is also comprised of many structural components. For example, a simple example of a bake shop will require, at the very least, to have an infrastructure allowing for creating a digital representation of the products – text, images, and so on. This is in addition to infrastructure required for storing, processing, and disseminating the digitized data. And, of course, there is a human component. Therefore, digitalization fits the definition of a complex system based on the complexity of its structure.

The second attribute is a *complexity of interactions* between the components – as long as digitalization includes a human component, it will exhibit patterns of non-linearity. But, even a purely technological system of digitalization would be bound to include some non-linear interactions between static parts – this is due to the law of diminishing returns and the absence of perfect scalability, where even intra-processor and RAM-processor interactions may exhibit patterns of non-linearity. After all, having 64 processing units available does not mean a 64-fold increase in processing speed. It would appear that digitalization qualifies as a complex system in terms of the presence of non-linear interactions between its components.

The third attribute is a *complexity of behavior* – digitalization is characterized by internal (intra system) and internal-external (inter/extra system) interactions that are hardly linear. In the case of our example, the undertaking would require a basic network architecture to connect all the required internal infrastructure, plus, an access to the Internet. Additionally, some sort of communication channels with customers and organizations handling shipping and banking must be established and maintained. This gives us sufficient support to qualify digitalization as a type of a complex system.

Research note: it seems reasonable to expect that researchers investigating digitalization-related subjects would explicitly state their meta-theoretical perspective on the subject. For example, within the same context digitalization could be viewed through the lens of CST as a social system, as a socio-technical system, as a technological system, as a revenue-generating system, as a power system and a tool of oppression, or as an organism. Different perspectives will result in very different findings and interpretations.

Let us consider the implications of stating the perspective on digitalization explicitly. An investigator may mention, for example, that "in this study we conceptualize digitalization as a socio-technical system and we view digitalization through the lens of complex systems theory". Such statement would, immediately, make it clear to all readers what the system consists of (e.g., social and technical components), what sort of interactions are there (e.g., non-linear interactions), and how the system behaves (e.g., complex behavior due to the internal interaction). Similarly, it is possible to view digitalization differently – an investigator may state that "we approach digitalization as a social system and the selected perspective is mechanistic", which immediately tells a reader that digitalization, as a system, is comprised of human components (e.g., people, groups, departments, etc.) that have assigned fixed roles, and the interactions between the components are linear.

Overall, there is an undeniable benefit in viewing digitalization as a complex system, because it allows, and, actually, forces an investigator to explicitly consider important aspects of the system and of the relationship between the system and its environment. For example, by applying CST, a researcher must explicitly consider:

1. The diversity of heterogeneous components comprising digitalization and the non-linear interrelationships between the components, as well as the diversity of information flows the components enable
2. The environment that forces digitalization to adapt or perish, and the venues via which the response in the form of environmental impact is generated
3. The structural and behavioral changes that digitalization must undergo as a response to the pressures of its environment
4. The inevitable complexity of the structure and function of digitalization as a logical response to dynamic influences of the context
5. The presence of complex associations instead of simple linear causal relationships acting within the system as well as during the system-context interactions
6. The limited applicability of the traditional functionalist methods of systems development to planning, analysis and design of digitalization-focused projects and environments
7. The inevitable appearance of emergent properties and unexpected events that must be taking into consideration during project management initiatives focused on digitalization
8. And so on…

It is not expected, of course, that in any given study all of the consideration would be taken into account. However, the overall goal of the study, the scope of the problem at hand, the suggested solution(s) – all of the aspects will be enriched if the perspective of "digitalization is a complex system" is adapted.

READER NOTES

Main points of agreement	
Supporting arguments (why agree?)	
Main points of disagreement	
Supporting arguments (why disagree?)	
Illustrative scenarios	
Possible research problem	
Possible research questions	

3

Assessing the Present and Planning the Future

Conceptually, our inquiry is within the paradigm supported by *Complex Systems Theory and Chaos Theory*. Consistent with these perspectives is the view that an instance of *digitalization* refers to a *state of a system* within its context – the context being a larger system represented by its environment. Consequently, we can analyze its current state (via knowing *how* it works), and we can plan its future state (via understanding *why* it works the way it does).

Our attempt relies on a set of simple independent, yet interrelated propositions (P#), and their corresponding justifications (JP#), which we express according to the structure of the statements of hypothetico-deductive logic. Specifically, we concentrate on two aspects associated with *digitalization*:

- First, analysis of the current "as-is" situation (current state of digitalization), and
- Second, a planning of "to-be" situation (future state of digitalization).

Consequently, the first point deals with describing the system in terms of its components and the interactions between them. The second point is concerned with predicting the changes in structure and behavior of the system based on the path it is likely to take.

Furthermore, let us turn our attention to three problematic (as we see them) aspects brought about by the absence of a common structured definition and the ambiguity of meaning of *digitalization*. At this point, we lack a clear understanding of the:

1. *Structure* of the system (e.g., what is it? What does it consist of?) – this is relevant to assessment and planning aspects of digitalization.

DOI: 10.1201/9781003304906-3

Meaning, unless we clearly understand how the system is supposed to function, we cannot determine whether digitalization functions correctly and properly, or whether there is something wrong and out of order.

2. *Scope of the impact* within which the system is intended to operate (e.g., what is the context? What is the environment within which the structure supposed to function?) – this is also relevant to assessment and planning aspects of digitalization. Simply put, if we don't know what the target of the impact of digitalization is, then we cannot assess whether the impact of digitalization is in line with what is expected by the target.

3. *Mechanism of the impact* by which the system effects its context (e.g., how does it work? What is the mechanism by which the structure impacts the context?) – this is of primary importance to the planning aspect of digitalization. Simply, if we aim for digitalization to be able to adapt its impact as a response to changes in the future, then we must know how, exactly, the impact is generated.

This is somewhat similar to answering the questions of the following scenario:

> *At this point in time, little Mary is a very talented and musically-inclined child.*
> *But, what would happen to Mary when she grows older?*
> *What can we do to help Mary to become successful in the area where her talents lie?*

And if we are interested in helping little Mary, then the three following points should be raised and must be addressed, as follows:

1. It is not clear what, exactly, Mary is talented at and, more importantly, with what set of available to her tools – does she have an outstanding physical ability? Does she have a good sense of music, but no physical ability? Or, does she differentiate, easily, "good music" from "bad music"? What does, specifically, "talented little Mary" mean?

2. It is not clear at what level of granularity Mary is good and talented – is Mary good at the level of a single instrument (e.g., voice), or a set of instruments (e.g., orchestra), or music in general (e.g., melody, composition, harmony, etc.)?

3. It is not clear what, exactly, Mary could do to progress in the area she is good at. Meaning, how to apply Mary's set of tools to the appropriate level of granularity at which her tools are the most appropriate? Does she have to learn how to sing? How to play an instrument? How to write/compose? Or, does she have to wait until she can write well so she could become a music critique?

At this point, we offer our reader an opportunity to examine the veracity of the propositions that support this inquiry, as well as to assess the corresponding justifications.

P1: Digitalization is a complex system.
JP1:
Major Premise: A complex non-linear dynamic system is a system comprised of a large number of components interacting in a non-linear way and capable of changing its state over time.
Minor Premise: Digitalization is a system comprised of a large number of components interacting in a non-linear way and capable of changing its state over time.
Conclusion: Digitalization is a complex system.
P2: Digitalization has a state.
JP2:
Major Premise: A life span of a complex non-linear dynamic system can be represented by a sequence of time-dependent states, such as if given a time period $T_1 \rightarrow T_2$, the system will transition from $SystemState_{(T1)} \rightarrow SystemState_{(T2)}$
Minor Premise: Digitalization is a complex non-linear dynamic system.
Conclusion: A life span of digitalization can be represented by a sequence of time-dependent states.
P3: The state of digitalization is context-dependent.
JP3:
Major Premise: A state of a complex dynamic system is the result of the interaction between the system and its environment, such as the time point T_n the system will reside in the $SystemState_{(Tn)}$ that is dependent on $EnvironmentState_{(Tn)}$
Minor Premise: Digitalization is a complex non-linear dynamic system.
Conclusion: A state of digitalization is dependent on the state of the environment.
P4: The state of digitalization is represented by its behavior and architecture.

JP4: Major Premise: A state of a complex dynamic system is represented by its behavior and architecture, such as the time point T_n the system will reside in the SystemState$_{(Tn)}$ characterized by SystemBehavior$_{(SystemStateTn)}$ and SystemArchitectu re$_{(SystemStateTn)}$

Minor Premise: Digitalization is a complex non-linear dynamic system.

Conclusion: A state of digitalization is characterized by its behavior and its corresponding architecture.

P5: A state of digitalization can be known by analysis – through the process of a hierarchical decomposition of a system into a set of components and their interactions.

JP5:

Major Premise: A state of a complex system can be known by analysis

Minor Premise: Analysis is a process of a hierarchical decomposition of a system into a set of components and their interactions

Conclusion: A state of a complex system can be known by decomposition of a system into a set of components and their interactions.

In regard to P5 it is important to note that while we can *know* the system via analysis, we cannot *understand* it via analysis – that would require synthesis.

The preceding five propositions suggest that at any given moment we should be able to know, by means of analysis, the state of digitalization via knowing its corresponding architecture and behavior (e.g., based on its attractor associated with the state of the system). The next three propositions deal with the subject of planning a state of digitalization – planning its future architecture and behavior.

P6: A future state of digitalization is dependent on the state of its environment.

JP6:

Major Premise: A future state of a complex system is dependent on the state of its environment, such as at the time point T_n the system will have a corresponding SystemState$_{(Tn)}$

Minor Premise: Digitalization is a complex non-linear dynamic system.

Conclusion: A future state of a digitalization is dependent on state of its environment.

P7: A state of digitalization can be planned to the extent to which a future state of its environment could be planned (predicted).

JP7:

Major Premise: A state of a complex dynamic system can be planned – its state could be manipulated to accommodate for future changes in its environment.

Minor Premise: Digitalization is a complex non-linear dynamic system.

Conclusion: A future state of a digitalization could be planned.

P8: Digitalization can become chaotic.

JP8:

Major Premise: According to Chaos Theory, complex non-linear dynamic systems are capable of exhibiting chaotic pattern of behavior

Minor Premise: Digitalization is a complex non-linear dynamic system.

Conclusion: Digitalization is capable of exhibiting chaotic pattern of behavior.

The last three propositions deal with the planning aspect of the state of digitalization, where we can plan a future state of digitalization, but only to the extent to which we can plan or forecast its future context. Also, if a future state of digitalization is to be planned, then it is important to keep in mind that the future state could become characterized by a chaotic behavior of the system. And if this is so, then the design of digitalization must explicitly consider some ways of addressing the issues of management of such emergent behavior.

The summary provided in Table 3.1 allows us to formulate a set of questions that we are planning to tackle in the upcoming chapters:

- *What are the structural elements of digitalization?*
- *What are the interactions between the structural components of digitalization?*
- *What are the intended outputs of digitalization?*
- *What is the context of digitalization?*
- *What are the intended targets of digitalization?*
- *What are the intended outcomes of digitalization?*
- *What are some of the ways of preventing digitalization from behaving chaotically?*

As our reader may notice, the stated above questions are not unique to the subject of this inquiry. Quite contrary – the same set of questions could be applied to any of the commonly used technical and socio-technical artefacts. For example, we can get clear answers to the questions in the case of cars, computers, coffee makers, video games, organizational information

TABLE 3.1

Problems and Requirement in Planning and Analysis of Digitalization

Purpose	Tool	Requirements	Current Problem
Assessment of the state of digitalization	Analysis	Structure of the system is known • Components • Inter-component interactions	The components of the system are not clearly stated The interactions between the components are not outlined
		Behavior of the system is known • Output of the system	The output of digitalization is not defined
Planning the future state of digitalization	Synthesis	Forecast of the system's context • Components • Interactions between components	The current context of digitalization is not defined The demands of the context on digitalization are not defined
		Forecast of the behavior of the system • Outcome produced by the system	The results of digitalization are not defined

systems. We do not have clear answers, however, in the case of the things and constructs denoted by such *hype words* as "business intelligence", "cybersecurity", "digitalization", "platformization", and so on.

This does not mean that such situation does not exist outside of the fields of IS/IT – quite the opposite, and one can locate a plethora of widely used terms referring to social, technical, and socio-technical constructs that float around with unclear structure, undefined context, ambiguous purpose and never mentioned evaluation criteria. "Green energy", "social justice", "police brutality", "healthy living", and so on – we are sure our reader could easily add a few more to the list. We do not make any judgments regarding such terms in any way or form, and this is not because possible issues that they portend to raise are valid or invalid, but it is because it is not clear what the terms mean.

READER NOTES

Main points of agreement	
Supporting arguments (why agree?)	
Main points of disagreement	
Supporting arguments (why disagree?)	
Illustrative scenarios	
Possible research problem	
Possible research questions	

4

Assumptions Underlying Structure of Digitalization

We cannot discuss any issues associated with the system's context without having a clearer idea than we currently have about the system itself. Consequently, let us make an attempt to outline, broadly, a complex dynamic non-linear system called *digitalization* – we shall do so by identifying essential components that digitalization *must* possess and functions that digitalization *must* perform. How are we to go about doing that? Well, our everyday experiences and common sense could guide us in the process.

Let us consider, as an example, a *vehicle*. There are many things around us that we refer to, for one reason or another, as vehicles. We can define a vehicle as a *technological artefact created for the purpose of transporting a cargo*, where *transporting* means *changing a spatial (e.g., geographic) location*, and *cargo* stands for *a bounded three-dimensional matter*, such as people or goods.

From a structural perspective, the essential components of a vehicle are:

1. Cargo placement area
2. Interface between the cargo area and the transportation surface
3. System controlling the interface

For all intents and purposes, the three structural components of a vehicle must be present in *any vehicle* because they are necessary for any object that we refer to as vehicle. Soft seats, radio, air conditioning could be there, but they are not essential to the function of a vehicle. Similarly, from the perspective of a *function* of a vehicle, we can also state that the essential

DOI: 10.1201/9781003304906-4

functionality of a vehicle – transporting a cargo – is based on the presence of the capabilities allowing the system (or its operator) to:

1. Load/unload a cargo
2. Move a cargo to a new location
3. Control the movement.

Conceptually, all and any vehicles in this world must possess the same essential structural components, and the same functionality. However, the *actual design and implementation* are specific to the perspective that underlies our assumptions regarding the vehicle. The following assumptions (e.g., *a vehicle is a...*), for example, would result in very different designs and implementations:

1. Vehicle is a *tool* allowing to do work
2. Vehicle is an *investment item*
3. Vehicle is a *sentiment*
4. Vehicle is a *source of pleasure*
5. Vehicle is an *object of art*.

Similarly, before we consider what digitalization is and what digitalization should do for us, we need to figure out the foundation on which digitalization is constructed.

As a result, we preamble this undertaking by presenting to our reader the basic assumptions (*A#*) underlying digitalization, followed by their corresponding justifications (*AJ#*) – this structure should guide the process of identifying what digitalization is and what it should do and make it transparent for our reader's analysis. To this end, digitalization rests on, or supported by, nine assumptions – we present the assumptions in Table 4.1 so our reader can examine their structure, meaning, and justification. Recall that our reader does not have to agree with the content of Table 4.1. Instead, we invite our reader to generate her own well-reasoned take on the matter.

The stated above assumptions allow us to provide general conceptual characteristics and associated implications of digitalization – we do so in Table 4.2.

Overall, it is fair to say that digitalization, as we know it today, rests on two following perspectives:

1. *Digitalization is a system of using a tool allowing to do work*
   Specifically, if we apply a definition of work as of *a process of applying energy to matter in order to transform the properties of the matter,*

TABLE 4.1

Justification of the Assumptions Underlying Digitalization

Assumption	Meaning	Justification
A1: *Production-oriented* *economic development*	Economic development is based on production of traded goods and services	*AJ1:* It is fair to say that there is a consensus regarding the essential role of economic development being a driver of socio-economic development, and the major source of economic development comes from the trade (internal as well as external) in resources – goods and services produced by an economy
A2: Productivity-based *economic progress*	Technological progress increases productivity, which serves as a driver of economic growth	*AJ2:* Any economic growth achieved by purely allocative means (e.g., via continuous increase in allocation of resources to achieve greater levels of production) faces a steep hill formed by the law of diminishing returns. Resultantly, there is a continuous pressure of improving the level of productivity via improving the state (rate and quality) of production of goods and services
A3: *Pursuit of effectiveness* *and efficiency*	Gains in effectiveness and efficiency are manifestations of increased productivity	*AJ3:* Productivity is commonly expressed in terms of effectiveness and efficiency, or, in the form of *Doing things right + Doing the right things*
A4: *Techno-centricity of* *improvements*	Mechanization and automation of the tools of production of goods and services are preferred routes leading to gains in effectiveness and efficiency	*AJ4:* One of the most established ways of increasing effectiveness and efficiency of business processes (by means of which goods and services are produced) is via technology – specifically, by means of mechanization of physical labor component of the business process (e.g., robotics), and automation of the decision-making component of the business process (e.g., algorithmic allocation of resources and AI-based pathing)

(Continued)

TABLE 4.1 *(Continued)*

Justification of the Assumptions Underlying Digitalization

Assumption	Meaning	Justification
A5: *Orientation on elimination and substitution*	Increases in effectiveness and efficiency are obtained by means of elimination and substitution of less effective and efficient methods	AJ5: Business processes obtain gains in effectiveness and efficiency via eliminating non-value producing activities (e.g., going lean), where only necessary value-adding activities and sub-processes remain. Further gains are possible only by replacing (substituting) remaining components of business processes with their more efficient counterparts. One of the "hard to substitute" components are those involving human judgment, intelligence, and inductive decision making
A6: *Mechanistic perspective*	Human cognition and decision making are computational in nature	AJ6: The field of computer science, which is the basis for complex computerized mechanization and automation of work, is based on mechanistic perspective – a view that human thinking/intelligence can be formalized and consequently expressed in the form of computer programs
A7: *Representational access to reality*	Access to real world is dependent on whether the subject of interest can be represented in some objective form, and what cannot be represented cannot be accessed.	AJ7: Computer science is founded on principles of positivism – where sensory (e.g., represented) data is manipulated via reason and logic. In the case of computer science the data is representation of reality and the reason and logic are embedded in, or expressed in the form of, computer programs
A8: *Symbolic modeling*	Things in real world could be objectively represented – modeled, by means of artificial constructs – symbols	AJ8: Fundamentally, computer science is concerned with theory of computation, and theory of computation deals with manipulation of symbols
A9: *Binary symbolism*	A bit is a preferred symbol of representation	AJ9: Binary digits are the elements of binary arithmetic, which underlies computation as it is currently implemented in computer science

TABLE 4.2

Implications of Characteristics of Digitalization

Conceptual Characteristic	Conceptual Implication
Structurally, digitalization is an interface	Digitalization is expected to be as simple as possible, and as transparent as possible, where a presence of more than a single layer indicates unnecessary complexity
Functionally, digitalization is a system for utilizing a digital-to-analog and analog-to-digital converter	Digitalization is expected to be as efficient as possible and as effective as possible, any losses of information are indicative of the presence of functional imperfections
Pragmatically, digitalization is an access point to value	Digitalization is expected to have no value per se, and to be "non-invasive" and transparent, where any incurred costs of using it are indicative of transactional imperfections

then we can define digitalization as a *system for using a tool allowing application of electrical energy to data with the purpose of transforming properties of the data.*

In this context "work" does not connote "labor", but stands for *any activity of interest to the user.* For example, a digital recording of a family gathering, done for pleasure and personal consumption, involves the same type of work as a digital recording of a lecture that is meant to be sold to its intended audience.

2. *Digitalization is a system for using the interface allowing an access to a value*

Similarly, if we use a definition of an interface as *a medium allowing for the interaction of the heterogeneous systems* (components), then we can define digitalization as a *system for accessing a medium allowing for translating economic resources (e.g., money) into an outcome of utilization of economic resources*, so that the perceived value of the outcome is greater than the perceive value of the expended economic resources. Let us consider a simple illustrative example. A person who creates a digital recording of his family reunion exchanges, for all intents and purposes, her available resources – time and energy, for another resource – a digital recording, because the perceived value of the recording is greater than the value of time and energy that was spent to make a recording.

At this point we are ready to consider the essential structural components of digitalization – we do so in the next chapter.

READER NOTES

Main points of agreement	
Supporting arguments (why agree?)	
Main points of disagreement	
Supporting arguments (why disagree?)	
Illustrative scenarios	
Possible research problem	
Possible research questions	

5

Essential Structural Components of Digitalization

Based on the information synthesized in the previous chapter, we can postulate the existence of three essential technological *structural components* of digitalization, plus a required communication channel (see Table 5.1). The components allow a user to instantiate the technological sub-system of digitalization, much in the same way as a driver of a car starts the vehicle and begins using it for her purposes. Thus, a user is also an essential part of the system, but, while the technological components have their functions enabled by their structure, a user does not have a function or a purpose within the system he or she is using. Instead, the user has a goal, which is obtaining value, and the value is generated by using a mechanism of conversion of analog data into digital data.

It is worth noting that the structural components we identify are not *physical* components, but the *conceptual* design elements. Consequently, every conceptual element could be implemented via a variety of *physical* designs. As a result, an instance of digitalization could be represented by a user accessing a single device containing all three design elements within a single housing, while another instance of digitalization could be exemplified by a user accessing a decentralized organization comprised of multiple employees supported by a complex distributed IT architecture.

But, despite the perceived differences, two systems of digitalization are *conceptually identical* because they are supported by the same set of essential components and they serve the same essential purpose. Hence, from this perspective, a digitalization initiative implemented by a multinational corporation to sell its products and services is not much different from a digital voice recorder purchased by a customer to play back the recording of a meeting.

DOI: 10.1201/9781003304906-5

TABLE 5.1

Essential Units of Digitalization

Essential Unit	Essential Purpose	Mechanism
Symbol generator	Generation of symbols by means of digital representation	Analog-to-digital conversion and pure digital generation
Symbol transmitter	Symbols-to-signal conversion	Generation of signals based on an encoding scheme
Symbol processor	Processing of the symbols using rules of logic	An operation of logic gates (transistors) as a result of passing of electromagnetic signals
Communication channel	Transmission of symbols by means of signals	A propagation of electromagnetic signal via transmission media

Another important point of note is that three essential structural components are *necessary and sufficient* for implementing digitalization. As a result, we can conceptualize digitalization, from a purely technical point of view, as a simple system. As a matter of fact, the best example of the technological sub-system of digitalization is a *scanner*. And, furthermore, using a scanner is a *gold standard* of what using digitalization should be, it is an *ideal* to be emulated by *any* instance of digitalization. A photographer who is using digital camera to take pictures or videos and to subsequently sell them (or to benefit from them in some other way of form) is another obvious example of digitalization.

Note of importance: this holds, of course, only in the case if we view digitalization as an interface and a tool allowing to do work and to access value. If, however, we view digitalization from a different perspective – let us say, as an interface that is a source of pleasure, then we must include additional, non-essential components geared towards delivery of whatever we define the pleasure is. For example, we would need to allow a person to take his/her own picture, and to be able to edit and modify the picture to her liking. This situation is not entirely unlike when a person purchases a work truck and proceeds to modify it by adding a set of fancy wheels, chrome accents, fancy audio system, and custom paint job. All those additions, while being a source of pleasure to the owner, are structurally and functionally unnecessary to the truck from the perspective of its intended purpose.

This has an important practical implication – if a design of digitalization must aim for approaching a simplicity of using a scanner or digital camera, then any design relying on more than three conceptual technical components must be deemed inefficient, and any presence of a human element in the implementation of digitalization (not counting the user) is indicative of inefficiency of the implementation of the system. This point is worth elaborating further.

So, from one point we have an idealized design of digitalization that is based on three essential components and those components are linked in a linear deterministic fashion. Consequently, what we have, as a result, is a good design implemented in the form of a simple device. But, we made an argument earlier that digitalization is a complex system – how do we reconcile the situation where the "as-is" system is a complex one, while an idealized "to-be" system should be a simple one?

The answer is straightforward – *the relative complexity of digitalization emerges as a response to ineffectiveness and inefficiency of the system as a whole, as well of the systems' components in particular.* Specifically, the increase in relative complexity of the structure and behavior of digitalization is due to the presence of the social (read, human) component, whose introduction into the system is necessary to alleviate the ineffectiveness and inefficiency of the technical components of digitalization. Clearly, the process of taking pictures using a digital camera could be easily automated (e.g., take a picture by using a timer or a photo element as a trigger to a movement), but in a lot of cases the resultant digital images may not be sellable to the public due to the absence of artistic value that the human actor – the photographer – generates.

Let us consider a simple illustrative example of a production line. If we have a fully automated production line functioning in a well-structured static environment, then it could be mechanically, electrically, and electronically *complicated*, but it will not be, for obvious reasons, *complex*. If, however, we do not have a fully automated line because we do not yet have technology to mechanize and automate certain functions performed by people, or because it is still cheaper to use people than to use machines, then we end up with a *complicated and complex* set up. Simply put, in the context of our elaboration on digitalization *complexity is a price to pay for not yet being able to eliminate the human component*, it is a price to pay for inefficiency caused by humans having their own self-interests. In other words, complexity is caused by *humans not being machines*. Or, more accurately, *the complexity of digitalization is caused by the failure of technology to duplicate relevant human abilities.*

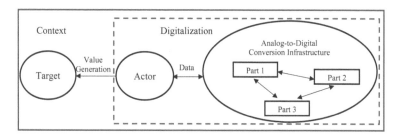

FIGURE 5.1
Digitalization and its context.

At this point in time, therefore, what is commonly referred to digitalization is a complex system implemented with a lot of technical components and characterized by plenty of social interactions (see Figure 5.1). We can consider, at this point, a route for reducing the structural complexity of digitalization, which is due to two factors: a large number of parts comprising the system, and a correspondingly large number of complex interactions between the parts. A common sense approach to accomplish such goal is via reducing the number of the parts comprising the system, which automatically results in reduction of the communication channels between the parts. This, inevitably, would result in the decrease of the relative complexity of digitalization, thus transforming it in the process from being a complex system to being a fairly simple machine. And, after all, using a simple machine is what digitalization should be.

Let us now look at the relative complexity of the structural components of digitalization, which is needed to identify the current and future limitations of the state of digitalization. In order to do that, we will take a look at the simplest and the most complex scenarios involving digitalization. Again, we are not going to concentrate on the interactions between the parts, because, as we argued before, as the complexity and the number of the components is going down, so does the number of interactions between them. Thus, fundamental structural limitations of digitalization are primarily component-, and only secondly interaction-based.

Simplest scenario of digitalization is using a scanner that allows for analog-to-digital (A2D) conversion of a drawing – but this is a "one-way street". Ideally, a perfect scanner would be a "two-way street" (e.g., modem, codec, etc.) capable of scanning an image of an analog drawing, converting it into a digital format, and converting the digitized image back into its original analog form without any loss of information. One of the approximations of such "scanner" is a digital voice recorder that allows a person to record a human speech, store it, and play it back when needed (albeit, with an inevitable loss of information). Another example is a pen-enabled tablet that allows for digitalizing of a hand-written note, storing it in a digital format, and displaying or reading it back in a what appears to be an analog format.

A more complex scenario involves digitalization being used to sell perfume on-line, where person will be able to smell the scent of a new fragrance without leaving her residence. In a similar fashion, it is not difficult to imagine digitalization allowing a person to sample a cookie via "digital cookie scanner" before buying a package on-line. But if we take the development of such scenarios to the limit, then the most complex instance of digitalization would be able to take the most complex analog thing known to man – a human brain, and to convert it into its digital representation, and then to re-convert it back into its original analog state.

Keeping the scenarios in mind, we can easily see digitalization at work in the simplest case. We can sort of see it in more complex scenario, but we cannot, really, see how it could work in the case of a human brain. Why not? If we consider a context of a space exploration, then we can easily relate to a spaceship being sent to the Moon, we also can conceive of a flight to other planets of the Solar system, and it is not inconceivable to imagine, plan, and design a space flight to other galaxies. Yes, it will be more expensive, yes, it will take more time, and so on, but, we can conceive of such undertaking. Why, then, it is a stretch to conceive digitalization being able to take human brain, convert it into digital format, and then convert it back to its original analog form? We can approach this problem in steps.

Let us consider the reasons for why, in a lot of cases, and even if we view digitalization as a tool and an interface, we cannot implement it via only three components. After all, we can conceptualize a "building" as a structure consisting of four walls, roof, and a floor, and we can actually design it that way, and we can implement it – construct it – that way. What stops us from implementing digitalization as a simple three-component machine? And, specifically, which component of digitalization is the most problematic one to implement and why?

Given our three-component (plus communication channel) structure of the technological sub-system of digitalization, it is easy to see that that the fundamental structural limitation of digitalization is associated with a *symbol generator* – the structural component dedicated to A2D and digital-to-analog (D2A) conversion (see Table 5.2). Once symbol generator

TABLE 5.2

Addressing Limitations of Essential Units of Digitalization

Essential Unit	Essential Limitation	Way of Addressing
Symbol generator	Information loss during analog-to-digital conversion	Via minimization of quantizing error, but *lossless conversion is not possible in principle*
Symbol transmitter	Synchronization of communication, symbol-to-signal distortion	By means of improvement in effectiveness and efficiency of encoding schemes
Symbol processor	Processing speed of CPU, system clock frequency, instruction set	Using massive parallelization/clustering, supercomputing, new designs (e.g., quantum computation)
Communication channel	Bandwidth of a channel & speed of transmission	Inverse multiplexing, parallel transmission, increasing bandwidth

produces a stream of bits, the bits could easily be processed by a processor and transmitted, where processing and transmission of digital data are relatively trivial, from engineering perspective, components. *Symbol transmitter* and *symbol processor* are the parts allowing for conceptualizing and implementing centralized or decentralized design of digitalization, nothing more – they are conceptually and technologically trivial components of digitalization. However, it is a *symbol generator* – the "interface of the interface", which is the most complex and problematic component of digitalization. The question to ponder on is *Why*?

Why is it that a symbol generator represents a stumbling block of digitalization? After all, what is so complex and sophisticated about A2D and D2A conversion? Do we not use it on an everyday basis, and do we not experience its seamless and problem-free implementation all the time in our lives? This becomes a question, really, of a type of a difference between analog and digital representation. Are they different *in kind*? Or, are they different *in degree*?

The very similar, in nature, question refers to the difference between humans and great apes – do we, humans, differ from apes in *kind*? Or, is at a difference in *degree*? Can we, hypothetically, take an ape and evolve it into human? If the difference is in kind, then the answer is no. If the difference is in degree, then we should be able to. Setting all the ethical issues aside, we can ask a question *If we cannot evolve an ape into a human then is this so because of the lack of resources, or is it so because it is impossible in principle?* This is, for all intents and purposes, a question relevant to a *quality of a conversion of a message between the formats.*

Now, placing our conversation back into the context of digitalization, the question becomes *whether the lossless A2D conversion is possible.* According to our current state of knowledge, such feat is not achievable due to the inevitable presence of the quantizing error, and it is not achievable in *principle.* Consequently, a major structural limitation of digitalization, and, therefore, the major limitation of an application of digitalization, is associated with an inherent imperfection of A2D conversion done by symbol generator. This brings us to the following propositions:

1. *The extent of utilization of digitalization is determined by a degree to which the context of digitalization is willing to tolerate the loss of information associated with A2D conversion.*
2. *The output of digitalization is a result of the functioning of the given structural state of digitalization.*

These two propositions are fairly intuitive – according to the first one, we use digitalization as long as we are satisfied with the inevitable imperfections of the deliverable, which we can express as the following equation:

$$Requested\_Output_{Digitalization} = Generated\_Output_{Digitalization}(Structure_{Digitalization})$$

And according to the second one, digitalization delivers the result of the conversion to the extent to which its structure allows it to do. The important thing to note is that we can express the structure of digitalization as a combination of two components – technical and social, in the following form:

$$Structure_{Digitalization} =$$
$$\left(Str\_TechComponent_{Digitalization} + Str\_SocialComponent_{Digitalization}\right).$$

But, this raises an important question, namely:

Why does the structure of digitalization need a social component?

After all, it is the social component that brings the problematic complexity to digitalization, with all the resultant consequences. Ideally, we would like to have the following relationship:

$$Requested\_Output_{Digitalization} =$$
$$Generated\_Output_{Digitalization}(Str\_TechComponent_{Digitalization})$$

Which means that the requested output is a result of the process of A2D conversion done by the symbol generator, and the better, technologically speaking, the symbol generator is, the better the generated output will be.

A possible answer is as follows:

> The social component is needed when the requested output of digitalization should be a representation of higher quality than the one generated by the technical component alone.

Meaning, what is produced by a technical component is not sufficient, not good enough – something else is needed. For example, a customer purchasing a box of cookies on-line wants not only to see images of cookies, but also wants to know how the cookies taste and smell.

This leads us to two implications:

1. *Social structural component of digitalization is a moving target for elimination via substitution by the technical structural component*
2. *Social structural component of digitalization will not be eliminated as long as:*
   a. *There is no technology capable of substituting the social component, or*
   b. *It is cheaper to use social component than a comparable technical component.*

At this point, we move our discussion to the topic of the functionality of digitalization, which deals with answering the question "What does it do?"

READER NOTES

Main points of agreement	
Supporting arguments (why agree?)	
Main points of disagreement	
Supporting arguments (why disagree?)	
Illustrative scenarios	
Possible research problem	
Possible research questions	

6

Functionality of Digitalization

At this point in our consideration we are ready to take a look at what, specifically, the structural elements of digitalization, taken separately as well as together, supposed to do. Simply put, if digitalization is a complex socio-technical system geared towards creating new business models and new information channels, then the *purpose* of digitalization is to *generate value*, which is fulfilled via the reliance on the functionality of the system to produce its *output* (see Figure 6.1).

This is similar to considering a modern car, comprised of hardware and software, being used by a driver/passenger. Together they represent a complex socio-technical system that exists for a single purpose of generating a value of some sort – this could be business, pleasure, any purpose that the passenger may consider when using the car. And the value is inevitably provided by the functionality of "car-driver" system that is obtained via emerging properties arising from the interactions between the social and the technical components of the system.

So, in an ideal scenario a car is operated by an auto-pilot driving system capable of taking commands from a passenger (or, ideally, knowing what the passenger wants without any interaction requiring active participation of the passenger) and interpreting them in such a way that the navigation route is found and the car is driven along the route to its destination. However, in a modern car we lack such functionality, and, consequently, we have to introduce a human element – a driver. As a result, we have a socio-technical system "car and driver" that operates within a given context for the purposes of satisfying the demands of an external system – its passenger. Clearly, a single physical actor could play both logical roles simultaneously – Joe could be the "driver" and "passenger" in the same time, or Joe could be the "driver" and Mary could be the "passenger" of the same vehicle.

DOI: 10.1201/9781003304906-6

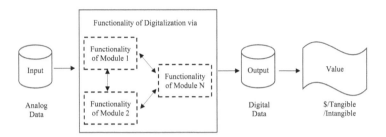

FIGURE 6.1
Digitalization and generation of value.

The overall functionality of digitalization, similarly, is achieved through the reliance on the emerging properties of the system that arise as a result of the interaction of the respective functionalities of its components.

This chapter requires us investigating the answer to the question of:

What is the functionality of digitalization?

For all intents and purposes, if we define functionality as an *ability to produce an output*, then this is the question of identifying the intended *output* of digitalization as well.

We start by defining essential *functions* of the structural components of digitalization, as well as the mechanisms by which the functions are implemented.

Let us note again, that *the presence of a human component is not an essential requirement of digitalization* – it is only going to be present if one of the essential components is, in some way, ineffective and/or inefficient. Consequently, an ultimate goal of digitalization, from the standpoint of its architecture, is to allow for generating value for its users without relying on a social component. Now that we have identified the essential functions of the essential components of digitalization, we can outline a typical scenario of value generation via digitalization, as presented in the Figure 6.2.

Based on this scenario, we can outline the intended functionality of digitalization, as follows:

> The functionality of digitalization lies in its ability to generate a digitized representation of a real-world object.

And this functionality is *obtained by means of the interactions of the structural components of digitalization* – symbol generator, symbol

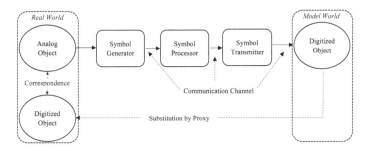

FIGURE 6.2
Scenario of value generation using digitalization.

transmitter and symbol processor connected by a communication channel. Interestingly, the seemingly more appropriate definition of the intended functionality of digitalization would be:

> The functionality of digitalization lies in its ability to generate value for its context from a digitized representation of a real-world object (see Table 6.1 and Figure 6.3).

However, under no circumstances digitalization is capable to assure what is generated based on the digitized representation is of value to its context. If this were the case, then all digitalization-related initiatives would be a success. However, this is not the case – for *output does not equal outcome.*

Let us recall that the structural components of digitalization are conceptual/logical, where a single component could be implemented via a combination of multiple physical elements and systems. This is similar to

TABLE 6.1

Essential Functions of Digitalization

Essential Unit	Essential Function	Mechanism
Symbol generator	To create a representation of (analog) reality in digital domain	Scheme-based conversion of the analog data into its digital counterpart
Symbol transmitter	To provide logical-to-physical conversion of data into signals	Scheme-based encoding of the digital data into a stream of signals
Symbol processor	To manipulate digital data using a set of instructions	Instruction-driven changes in properties of digital data
Communication channel	To allow for propagation of signals between units	Analog or digital transmission of signals

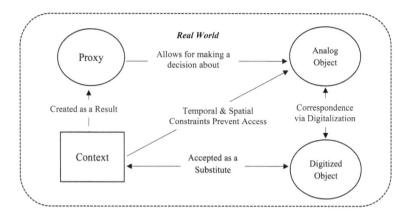

FIGURE 6.3
Expanded scenario of value generation using digitalization.

a computer processor, which is implemented as a system of interactions between an arithmetic-logic unit, control unit, set of registers, system clock and so on.

If we define *output* as *an end result of the process of transformation of inputs*, then we can state that:

> The output of digitalization is represented by data in digital format.

Let us consider another illustrative scenario, where a retailer wants to advertise and sell its latest offering, let us say, a pair of shoes, on-line. One of the components of "advertise and sell" initiative is associated with creating a digital representation (e.g., an image, or a video) of the real-world object – in this case, a representation of shoes. A perfect example of digitalization will follow a scenario with no human involvement – when a produced pair of shoes is placed, automatically, into a "digitalization box" that is capable of creating an *analog-to-digital* (A2D) representation of the pair of shoes in such a way, that the resultant digital data could be stored, transmitted, and, eventually, re-converted into the pair of shoes (or, their holographic representation coupled with the simulation of the tactile qualities of the pair) at the destination. A more sophisticated case of a multiplexer, of sorts…

From a perspective of a simpler case of digitalization, which is exemplified by the process of using a digital camera, the sequence of steps if fairly trivial – a picture is taken, processed, stored, and disseminated to a target location. It can be easily seen that the process could be completely automated (e.g., photo element to trigger the process) to maximize the efficiency of digitalization, and if the process is standardized and relies on a pre-defined set of specifications, then it allows for maximization of effectiveness of digitalization as well. So, in the case of our scenario, the duration of the process is the total time between the point t_1, when the button is pressed to take an image, and the point t_n, where the digital file of the image is saved in the memory. Same goes for cost of the process, where it is a combination of all the little costs involved during the period between t_1 and t_n.

In reality, however, the actual system of digitalization is far from trivial, because it is comprised of components and activities that take a disproportionally large amount of time, energy, and money to implement and to perform. For example, it is likely to take a much longer time to set up a shoot of the product (e.g., light, angle, background, etc.) then to take a picture itself. Also, once the picture is taken, it is likely that it will be modified by retouching the image – and this is also a very resource-consuming process. So, what we end up with is a system and its processes that *should be*, from a technological perspective, fast, inexpensive, and relatively simple. But, instead, we end up with the system and the processes that are complex, relatively slow, and expensive. A reasonable question to ask is *Why?*

A simple answer to this question is that *digitalization is used because its context requires a certain outcome*, and in a lot of cases a purely technical system supporting digitalization cannot deliver the desired outcome. Consequently, this discrepancy introduces a necessity for the human/social component of digitalization, where human presence is needed to attend to the tasks and responsibilities that the technical component is unable (or, not yet able) to provide. Let us now take a look at some of the routes by which the delivery of the output of digitalization could be improved.

READER NOTES

Main points of agreement	
Supporting arguments (why agree?)	
Main points of disagreement	
Supporting arguments (why disagree?)	
Illustrative scenarios	
Possible research problem	
Possible research questions	

7

Improving the Output of Digitalization via Process Optimization

Now, let us consider some of the ways of assessing the functionality of digitalization that results in production of the output. It is important to note that at this point we are not dealing with the *evaluation of the output* by the context – in this chapter we do not consider *outcomes* of digitalization. Instead, we dedicate our attention to the routes of *improving the output* – the data in a digital format. If we consider a process-oriented perspective, then there are two routes by which the output of a process could be improved – first, via improving the quality of inputs, and, second, by means of improving the process of transformation of inputs into outputs.

In our case, we consider inputs to digitalization to be "stable", "as-is", and non-negotiable – this is because the inputs simply represent a given state of the analog environment to be provided to digitalization for the consequent transformation. For example, if we want to use a scanner to digitize a complex drawing, then, intuitively, it is a more complex input than a simple drawing of a straight line or, of a rectangle. But, it makes no sense to attempt to simplify a complex drawing of a human body in motion by means of representing it, instead, via stick figure. Same goes for digitalization involving analog audio, or digitalization involving hard copies of accounting records – they are what they are, and no amount of improvement, via simplification or other means, will make analog signals be "closer" to their intended digital representations.

It is also worth noting that we are not concerned with pre-processing of analog data as a way of improving digitalization. This means that filtering out the background noise from the analog audio recording, or "cleaning up" accounting records prior to hard copy-to-digital processing are

TABLE 7.1

Factors Impacting Effectiveness and Efficiency of Digitalization

Functionality	Criterion	Definition	Factors Impacting Criterion
Producing a digitized representation of a real-world (analog) object	Efficiency	Degree of minimization of resources required for producing output	Time (How long it takes?) Cost (How expensive is it?)
	Effectiveness	Degree of success in producing output via compliance with the prescribed/requested specifications.	Control of the process via minimization of a variation Compliance with specifications established for every component of digitalization

not within the scope of this undertaking. Thus, we consider the *process improvement* as a viable route to improving the output of digitalization.

Specifically, let us consider two *characteristics* of the process by means of which digitalization implements its functionality and produces its output, namely, *efficiency of the process* and *effectiveness of the process* (see Table 7.1). In order to do so, let us consider each of the aspects, along with suitable criteria for the evaluation of the factors. It is worthwhile to note that we only consider the *execution* of the process – all issues relevant to the set up (e.g., planning, analysis, design, implementation) or a maintenance of the process are outside the scope of our consideration.

By identifying the criteria relevant to the assessment of the output, as well as by identifying relevant factors impacting the criteria, we are in a good position for assessing the routes by which the functionality of digitalization, as well as its output, could be improved. Let us consider some of the relevant factors in order.

If we consider implications of the information compiled in Table 7.2, then it is easy to see that improvements in functionality and the output of digitalization comprise a fairly trivial, from engineering and technological point of view, set of undertakings.

For example, if we consider using a scanner being a "gold standard" of digitalization, then it is very easy to design and implement improvements allowing a scanner to produce, faster and cheaper, digital images of an increasingly higher quality. It is important to note that we may decide against doing so for a variety of reasons – for example, it could be not

TABLE 7.2

Improving Functionality of Digitalization

Factor	Impacted by/Result of
Time	$t_{\text{A2D\_conversion}} + t_{\text{digital\_processing}} + t_{\text{digital\_transmission}} + t_{\text{signal propagation}}$
Cost	$\$_{\text{A2D\_conversion}} + \$_{\text{digital\_processing}} + \$_{\text{digital\_transmission}} + \$_{\text{signal propagation}}$
Process control	Predefined flow of digitized and digital data through the components
Specifications' control	Utilization of protocols, standards, encoding and conversion schemes

economical, or it may be that we are satisfied with the existent quality of digitalization, or because the digital product is already cheap enough.

Note: This could be a redundant point to make, but it is tremendously important to point out, again, the difference between the output of digitalization and the outcome of digitalization. For example, let us say, Company X adopted a digital platform to better serve its customers. For all intents and purposes, if we are interested in effectiveness of the new platform, then we must ask a question: An effectiveness of what, exactly? After all, it is conceivable that Company X goes out of business because its customers do not use the digital platform while the platform delivering an excellent output.

After all, it is perfectly clear that the effectiveness of the performance of digitalization, if seen as the process of producing a digital representation to generate a (possible new) value, is completely circumscribed, from a technological standpoint, by the process of A2D conversion. And the process ends when the analog data is converted into its digital representation and then sent out to its target destination to generate value. If this is so, then effectiveness of digitalization is dependent on selecting an appropriate encoding scheme, and constraining the process of conversion so it does not vary too much. Again, what is "too much" in terms of variation of the process is to be under purview of manufacturing specifications of a given system.

Consequently, the undertaking of researching *effectiveness of digitalization* amounts to comparing a desired quality of output with the actual output, and identifying the reasons for disparity. This could become a worthy enterprise, because such investigation could yield interesting results – we could discover that a current encoding scheme is sub-par (e.g., we cannot digitize the taste of chocolate), or, we could determine that the mechanism of conversion is lacking (e.g., we cannot record our dreams as digital videos), or, we could decide that such conversion is bound to fail because we lack the appropriate foundation (e.g., a problem of induction is not solved – digitalization cannot deal with novel situations), as an in the case where we want to convert a partially completed analog sketch into a completed digital picture/drawing. But, putting all the worthy and interesting discoveries along the way aside, we are bound to realize that the problem of effectiveness of digitalization is comprised of two components – a conversion scheme, and a mechanism of conversion.

Investigating issues of efficiency of digitalization is not much different in terms of complexity. For example, we could investigate a relative efficiency of a conversion scheme, where we would be concerned with minimizing the number of logical steps involved, and the efficiency of an algorithms at each step. Also, we could be interested in the relative efficiency of the conversion scheme as it applies to a particular platform – we could be interested to find out the number of physical primitives associated with each logical step. Or, we could descend all the way to the level of instruction set and be interested in efficiency of a processor involved in conversion. And while those are worthy subjects, they are better left under purview of math and computer science and computer engineering, because they deal with the tools, with the machinery involved in the process, and not the process itself.

In a similar way, if we are to investigate the aspect of relative efficiency of digitalization as it is impacted by the mechanism of conversion, then such undertaking is also reducible to studying time and cost of the process. Which, ultimately would always lead to a goal of complete automation of the process via elimination and substitution of a human component. And, if we are guided by mechanistic perspective, then this is absolutely achievable in all areas where we use digitization. It is just a matter of time before singularity strikes and computer programs duplicate human mind. But, Achilles never catches the tortoise if one operates on the basis of romantic perspective.

In the next chapters we look at some general impacts that digitalization will produce on its internal and external environment. Let us consider a general scenario of a complex dynamic system residing within a dynamic context of its environment. Within the scenario the system would be under the pressure of two outside forces. The first force is expansive, where the environment may offer some opportunities for the system to expand into the new areas – this is a "pull" force of the environment. The second force is compressive, where the environment exerts a pressure on the system to contract – it is a "push" force of the environment. The presence of both forces impacts digitalization and the effectiveness and efficiency of its processes – the forces apply pressures requiring digitalization to make a continuous and constant effort geared towards the process improvement. For example, a "pull" force may result in a successful expansion of digitalization only if the output of digitalization is effective – read, is in compliance with the requirements of the new contexts of expansion. Similarly, a "push" force will require the process to become exceedingly lean and void of inefficiencies. This is not entirely unlike the impact of globalization on modern businesses, which brought an additional attention to the process orientation and its corollaries – process efficiency and process effectiveness.

In the case of the both forces being active, digitalization is under a constant pressure of continuous remodeling – this will force the modularity of the structure, where the modules are expected to be highly cohesive and loosely coupled. The general implications are simple, and they are based on the continuous drive towards achieving fundamental qualities required for digitalization to survive by countering "push" forces and thrive via expanding by taking advantage of "pull" forces. We provide some considerations regarding the most obvious goals associated with such remodeling along with some of the methods for achieving the goals in Table 7.3.

We continue by considering the impact of digitalization on its internal environment – this is the subject of the next chapter.

TABLE 7.3

Methods for Increasing Effectiveness and Efficiency of Digitalization

Method	Drive Towards a Goal of	Possible Means
Simplification of the user's interface(s)	Elimination of the non-standard inputs	Using AI (e.g., chat bots) to elicit and to enforce standardized inputs
Simplification of the structure of the modules	Elimination of the human element	Using AI (e.g., scenario-based) to substitute human involvement at the level of the module
Simplification of the relationships between the modules	Elimination of the non-linear relationships between the modules	Incorporation of increasing number of pre-defined scenarios of increasing complexity
Simplification of the processing	Elimination of the non-algorithmic processing	Allowing only standardized inputs and using associated scenarios to handle them
Simplification of the decision making	Elimination of the discretionary decision making	Using AI to translate non-standard scenarios into an increasingly large number of standardized scenarios

READER NOTES

Main points of agreement	
Supporting arguments (why agree?)	
Main points of disagreement	
Supporting arguments (why disagree?)	
Illustrative scenarios	
Possible research problem	
Possible research questions	

8

Impact of Digitalization on Its Internal Environment

Let us consider a hypothetical scenario where digitalization is facing both "push" and "pull" pressures of the environment. An example of such scenario is a company that has two interrelated goals to pursue. First, the company aims to maintain (or, to increase) its share of the *same* segment of the customers on the market by providing, at the very least, the same level of quality of service to its customers, but at the increasingly higher levels of efficiency and effectiveness than the competitors offer (e.g., read, faster and cheaper without sacrificing required level of quality). Second, the company may want to decide to take an advantage of an opportunity and to expand into the *new* segments of the market by offering new types of A2D conversion services.

We must note that every specific internal context will have its own specific set up allowing for the delivery of the output, but, regardless of the context, the A2D conversion and the delivery of the digital data takes place along the general routes presented in Table 8.1. Overall, it is intuitive that improvements in efficiency and effectiveness of digitalization come from a simplification and a streamlining of its internal environment.

However, another scenario is also possible – let us consider a situation when a business aims to expand via providing new services via digitalization, and the new services go beyond what a "pure" digitalization in the form of A2D conversion can currently offer. For example, this could be a bakery, which allows an on-line service of ordering, processing, and consequent delivery of baked goods, but also decided to expand its business by means of offering a preparation of high-margin custom cakes. The "custom" part would require the presence of a human element in the process – even if the consultation regarding the product could take place via

DOI: 10.1201/9781003304906-8

TABLE 8.1

Impact of Improvements in Effectiveness and Efficiency of Digitalization

Impact	Internal Outcome	Justification
Minimization of the interface of symbol generator	Elimination and substitution of data/information acquisition staff	• Human involvement indicates inefficiency of the production process • Human involvement implies an extra layer of an interface to deal with (environment→ human→ digital vs. environment→ digital)
	Elimination or minimization of analog touch-points	• Any analog input to the system from an internal or external source must be digitized, which causes inefficiency in the process and must be minimized or eliminated
	Elimination of discretionary inputs	• Any discretionary inputs require extra processing (and, possibly, conversion from analog), causing inefficiency in the process
Information flow optimization	Elimination and substitution of information gaps in business processes caused by analog-based activities	• Speed of a business process is dependent on the speed of the movement of the data within the process, where information gaps and hand-offs cause inefficiencies to be eliminated
	Elimination of discretionary information channels	• Discretionary information channels introduce variance into a business process, which must be managed and controlled – this causes inefficiencies to be reduced or eliminated
	Centralization of information storage and complex processing	• Decentralization of complex decision making carries a penalty of managing dependencies and integration of the results of intermediate/parallel processing, and, thus, to be eliminated • Movement of data/information causes inefficiencies, thus, to be stored close to, or at the point of processing.
	Direct "center→ edge" and "edge→ center" channels	• Any intermediate nodes cause inefficiencies in information flow and data processing and are to be eliminated

(Continued)

TABLE 8.1 *(Continued)*

Impact of Improvements in Effectiveness and Efficiency of Digitalization

Impact	Internal Outcome	Justification
Automation of decision making	Elimination and substitution of the human operational and tactical-levels decision makers	• Standardization of decision making process via model-based scenarios allows for automated decision making, which increases efficiency of a business process
	Centralization of decision making	• Decentralized and flexible decision making structure causes inefficiencies in a business process and to be eliminated
	Elimination of discretionary decision making	• Discretionary decision making is needed in the case of deviations from the normal flow of a business process, which is caused by deviations from a "normal" set of models/scenarios, but it causes inefficiencies and to be eliminated
	Categorization- or classification-based decision making	• An efficient decision making is based on the algorithmic structure and clearly defined and categorized inputs – any deviations from established categorization will cause inefficiencies in decision making and to be eliminated

Skype, Zoom, or any other application of such type, the expensive human involvement is still there.

The result of such expansion would be a socio-technical system, which is, almost by definition, is technically inefficient. This will lead to two possible routes along which the business may want to proceed. First route is to make no changes and to keep the social component intact. The second route is by trying to eliminate the social component via eventual substitution. In the first case the business makes this inherent inefficiency the selling point for the business – it is the "human touch" that develops the business. Or, in the second case, the business proceeds via a well-paved route of automation and substitution that leads to an initiation and implementation of a business process by a customer via a sequence of clicks. There is, seemingly, no other ways of conducting the business. Based on the information synthesized in this chapter, we can forecast the developmental trajectory of a viable system of digitalization.

In one case, a system may decide to embrace *the presence of inefficiency in the form of a human component as a source of a competitive advantage.* For example, let us consider a custom shop of any sort – let us imagine that this is a business specializing in hand crafted knives. The competitive advantage of such business comes from two aspects – skilled trade and customization according specifications of each customer. So, it is possible that a certain part of the "order-make-buy" process could very well be digitalized. For example, a shop can display its catalog on line, a shop can send its clients sketches of the future products, and a shop can implement an on-line payment system. But, it is unlikely that the human sources of competitive advantage, such as in-person consultation (even if takes place over Skype or Zoom), will ever be moved to a digital domain. Furthermore, such type of a business is hard to scale, and the extent of the application of digitalization is impacted by the scalability of a business.

In another case, a system views *the presence of a human component as a source of inefficiency, and consequently, as a possible source of a competitive disadvantage.* As a result, such system selects to pursue a goal of simplification of its internal structure and architecture via elimination of the human component. If we continue with our example of a custom shop specializing in handcrafted knives, then we can imagine a scenario where the business may select to follow a route of (almost) complete digitalization. For example, once the shop discovers the global community of shoppers, then it may select to pursue a route of expanding its customer base by offering more "quasi-custom" options. Such path could be easily paved by digitalization via reliance on the customers to select the options from the drop-down boxes and lists of values. This will lead to increasing mechanization and automation of the production with the subsequent elimination and substitution of a human component that was once the source of the competitive advantage of the business. Such business may even choose to retain a "halo" product intended to bring in its fold the new customers desiring a truly custom item. However, an increasingly greater part of the business would follow the preferred route of digitalization guided by substitution and elimination of a human component. And this means consistently increasing implementation of mechanized and automated processes of production, and the associated upstream and downstream activities.

An interesting question to consider, however, is the following one. In the case of digitalization where remaining human component is considered to be a source of a sustainable competitive advantage, would the human component exert the pressures on the technical component with the purpose to minimize its involvement? And, as a corollary, what would determine the boundary of the co-existence of the two components? In the next chapter we take a look as some of the impacts that digitalization exerts on its context.

READER NOTES

Main points of agreement	
Supporting arguments (why agree?)	
Main points of disagreement	
Supporting arguments (why disagree?)	
Illustrative scenarios	
Possible research problem	
Possible research questions	

9

Impact of Digitalization on Its External Environment

We must note that every specific external context will have its own "flavor" or a "costume" in which the result is delivered, but, regardless of the context, the output is delivered along the general themes presented in Table 9.1.

Let us consider some typical scenarios associated with the "digitalization-to-context" set up. For all intents and purposes, digitalization, as a complex dynamic system, would aim to expand into its environment, and the expansion would be an opportunistic affair, and not a "hostile takeover". Furthermore, this expansion would be synergetic in nature – digitalization would not aim to "kill" or to diminish a viability of its "host". A simple example of expansion of telemedicine into rural communities demonstrates the process – digitalization of medicine does not aim to substitute in-person visits where such visits are available or unavoidable. Instead, a telemedicine, as a complementary service, will expand into the areas with a demand for medical services and the absence of in-person medical service.

But, importantly, only to the extent where it can substitute a "real thing" of an in-person visit. There will be no "how to do the surgery on your own" videos on YouTube, and we should not expect "This is how you read your MRI and X-Ray and Ultra Sound images" instructions on the websites of the hospitals. Thus, telemedicine in this case can be viewed as a resource fulfilling a demand, *to the acceptable extent*, where no alternatives are available. And because the interaction between digitalization and its environment is a three-part system, the growth of digitalization would show its impact on the appropriate components – its internal structure, its interface with the environment, and the environment itself. Let us consider those aspects in order.

DOI: 10.1201/9781003304906-9

TABLE 9.1

Impacts of Improvements of Digitalization on External Context

Impact	Impact on the Context	Justification
Interface minimization	Elimination and substitution of sales/customer service staff	• Standardization of external context will be based on introduction of category-based taxonomies, and will result in automation of the data inputs and information outputs of the system
Information flow optimization	Information deluge designed to overwhelm individual decision-making abilities	• Optimized channels allow for inexpensive, efficient and effective delivery of information from the system to its context • Delivery of relevant information increases inefficiencies in data flow and data processing parts of the system • By observing the process of culling of the information (selection of the relevant information) by the context more information about the context could be gained – this contributes to creation of a better model of the context by the system
Decision-making automation	Substitution of customer-centric internal decision making with digitalization-centric external algorithm/AI-based structure	• Customer-centric decisions made within the context of the system results in "pull" type of system-context interaction, which causes inefficiencies in production process due to variability in requirements • Accumulation of the information about the context (customers) results in generating better models of the context, which leads to better matching the output of the system with the outcome of the process • Context is becoming conditioned to receive "good enough" suggestions and "expert" recommendation, which leads to substituting local decision making of the context with the centralized decision making of the system

Regarding the environment – the expansion would come from two sources. First, digitalization would aim to acquire a larger share of the environment of *the same type*. For example, a company specializing in creating websites for small businesses would aim to increase the number of the clients of *the same type* – let us say, small businesses. In order to make this work, digitalization would have to become relatively cheaper, relatively easier to use, and to offer a greater value along the way. There is a simple path for making the services cheaper – via substitution and elimination of the human component on a social side, and via elimination and substitution of custom technical elements with off-the-shelf counterparts. This, in turn, would have to lead to commoditization of digitalization with all the logical consequences it entails.

Second, digitalization would aim to acquire a new territory by offering services to the environment of *a different type*. For example, a company specializing in creating websites for small businesses may expand into the area of customer resource management, and offer services allowing for tracking and serving the visitors of the sites that were created for the businesses. In the absence of turnkey modules to accommodate the new offerings, a new module would have to be created – with the necessary involvement of a human component. Thus, the emerging pattern is fairly clear – any growth and development of digitalization is corresponded by a wave-like pattern of acquisition, usage, and subsequent attrition of a human component.

Regarding the interface – the expansion would be enabled by the development of new interfaces allowing for accommodating a wider variety of contexts. The question, however, is regarding the general architecture of such interface – what would allow the interface to smoothly accommodate new contexts? Given the fact that it is the interface that is the point of A2D translation/representation, it is clear that such accommodation to the new context cannot take place by using only technical means. Instead, a human component is needed, even if it is going to be used temporarily. But, again, what is going to happen when a new interface has been created and is properly functioning to accommodate the new context? The answer is similar to the answer regarding the internal environment of digitalization – a human component of a new interface will face, in time, the process of substitution and elimination by its technical counterpart. An interesting problem, however, is identifying those components of a real world that could not be, in principle or by economic reasons, digitized automatically and, thus, require attention of a human component of the interface.

Regarding the context of digitalization – we need to keep in mind that it is comprised of two components. One component is analog, and it serves as an input to digitalization, and it is a supplied representation of the real world in the form of analog data. The second component is digital, and it is represented by digital consumers of digital data. The "input context" interested in utilizing digitalization would have to, actively or not, consciously or not, adjust to the new interface provided by digitalization. This means that this component will become conditioned to perceive (and present within the context) its analog reality in a "quasi-digital" format compliant with the interface of digitalization.

A good example of such adaptation is an acceptance of common A2D scales of representation and the associated discrete values by the general public, such as reliance in an ordinary everyday life on Likert-scale representations, standard color palette (e.g. white, black, brown, etc.), shoe and clothing sizes, and so on. It is undoubtedly true that humans are conditioned by the language they use, and it is in a similar way that the context of digitalization would become conditioned by the digital representation the system produces. For example, many software engineers and developers become conditioned to utilize algorithmic thinking outside of work, and musicians often perceive the sound they hear in terms of notes and scales.

The implications are fairly simple – a context of digitalization that supplies the analog data and receives digital data in return, would aim, eventually, to minimize the quantizing errors via adapting to digitalization and using some form of "analog censorship". Such activity is not unique to digitalization – it is simply a process that emerges naturally, because it results in the increased efficiency and effectiveness of obtaining the end result. For example, film photographers would be conditioned by their equipment and make a decision whether to take a picture on the basis of how well their equipment would accommodate the analog environment (e.g., "It is too dark here" or "Too much light"). Another easy example is provided by videoconferencing, where participants are often willing to sacrifice their real-world appearance for the benefit of looking good on a digital display.

READER NOTES

Main points of agreement	
Supporting arguments (why agree?)	
Main points of disagreement	
Supporting arguments (why disagree?)	
Illustrative scenarios	
Possible research problem	
Possible research questions	

10

Significance of Digitalization – Why Is It Important?

Based on the information presented in the previous chapters, we can the put forward yet another proposition:

Digitalization will aim to force standardization of its internal and external environment.

We offer the following justification for this proposition:

Major premise: Increase in efficiency and effectiveness of a process of production of goods or services is dependent of the standardization of the internal and external to the process contexts.

Justification: Standardization, or any purposeful decrease in the volatility and variability of a process, leads to minimization of deviation-related errors and contributes to the increases in efficiency and effectiveness of a process of production.

Minor premise: The goal of digitalization is to increase efficiency and effectiveness of production and delivery of goods or services.

Conclusion: Digitalization is dependent on standardization of the internal and external contexts.

At this point we are ready to consider the intended impact of digitalization, and we do so next.

The *impact* of digitalization is represented by the *gains in efficiency and effectiveness of business processes* of production of goods or services.

Note: It is important to point out that by *business processes* we do not mean only the *processes run by businesses* to produce goods and services. Instead, we view it as a *general process of delivering a perceived value*. Based on this definition, a person listening to a digital recording while commuting is also utilizing a business process to obtain a value delivered by that process.

DOI: 10.1201/9781003304906-10

TABLE 10.1

Impact of Essential Units of Digitalization

Essential Unit	Essential Function	Impact
Symbol generator	To create a representation of reality in digital domain	Minimization of A2D interface
Symbol transmitter	To create new or optimize existing information channels	Maximization of effectiveness and efficiency of information channels
Symbol processor	To automate information processing	Automation of decision making

Consequently, if we continue with mechanistic point of view, then the importance of digitalization is that it allows for a more efficient and effective delivery of products or services to the context. The significance of digitalization, then, is that it allows for reduction in resources dedicated to the process – it allows for maximizing the value via minimization of losses incurred by performing the process (see Table 10.1).

Earlier we raised an issue associated with the absence of a precise definition and the meaning of the term *digitalization*. A more serious issue than that of a *meaning* of a term is the issue of the *significance* of what the term stands for. This is because it involves an assessment of the *impact* of the defined construct on the system, and the assessment of the impact is important in planning the future of the system. Basically, this is an issue of posing and answering the question of *Why is this important?* An inquiry of such sort, clearly, leads to a slew of questions of the type:

- *What makes digitalization important?*
- *Could we make the impact of digitalization greater?*
- *How to plan on keeping digitalization being important in the future?*

Fundamentally, it is an issue of planning and strategizing, and it is a very common issue to many fields and industries. Let us consider any Department of Information Systems and Computer Science that is tasked with educating and preparing workforce for tomorrow's marketplace. It is commonly mentioned that the jobs that such graduates would apply for do not exist yet. In the same time, there is an agreement that a lot of careers and jobs in the areas of IS and CS would disappear in the next 5 or 10 years. So, in a similar fashion we could ask the questions like:

- *What make the graduates valuable to the current employers?*
- *What would make the graduates more valuable?*
- *How do we educate the graduates so they are valuable in the future?*

There is a good example of a planning-related problem associated with the utilization of a term with a well-defined structure and not-so-clearly understood significance – a prescription medication under the name of OxyContin. In this case, the term "OxyContin" stands for a chemical compound with a well-understood structure (e.g., 6-deoxy-7,8-dihydro-14-hydroxy-3-O-methyl-6-oxomorphine) – it is a pain-reliever drug, and its significance, its impact, lies in its ability to relieve pain in suffering individuals. However, it turns out that OxyContin is much more significant than was originally thought – there are other "impacts", at different levels, associated with its use (see Table 10.2). In order to save space, we save the reader details and just note that OxyContin epidemic is a well-known problems and is a widely accepted fact.

Another example is *high-fructose corn syrup* (HFCS) – an artificial sugar made from corn syrup that is commonly used to sweeten processed foods and soft drinks. Its definition and meaning are pretty straightforward – it is a sugar substitute that is an artificial sweetener. However, its impact, its significance, is not so easy to express. This is because, from one perspective, it is a low-cost sugar substitute, and it makes a good economic sense to use it in a food industry. But, from another perspective, many experts believe that HFCS is one of the key factors in today's obesity epidemic, partially culpable for diabetes and heart disease.

TABLE 10.2

Example of Context-Specific Outcome

OxyContin – Context	OxyContin – Outcome
Receptors	Binding to a receptor, inhibition of adenylyl-cyclase and hyperpolarization of neurons, and decreased excitability
Individual (Nervous system)	Pain relief
Individual (Human body)	Addiction
Society (many individuals)	Addiction epidemic

So, we have a system in its dynamic context – and the context derives the benefits from that system *at this point* and this what keeps the system alive. And we want to let the system grow and develop *in the future* to continue benefitting its context. However, this requires introducing changes, and not just sporadic *ad hoc* changes, but planned changes that are conducive to the orderly growth and development of the system. Consequently, given a fairly reasonable assumption that we want to implement *positive* changes to the system within its context, the question *Why is this important?* is bound to evolve into *Why is this beneficial?* and, in turn, *Who is the beneficiary?* This, inevitably, brings us to the necessity of defining the *context* of the impact. A complex dynamic system would tend to evolve towards equilibrium and stability, but the equilibrium and stability are contextual – a system in the state of equilibrium in one context is not necessarily in the same state if placed in a different context.

Consequently, let us take a look at the context of digitalization (see Figure 10.1). It could be presented as being comprised from two conceptual components: a module that provides analog data and a module that receives digital data. This take allows us to view digitalization as an information channel within the context, which connects a source module (e.g., analog data transmitter/source) and a destination module (e.g., digital data receiver/sink). Such perspective allows us to refer to Shannon's *Theory of Information* to get some additional insights into the system. For example, if digitalization is an information channel, then two things are obvious from the get go: digitalization is impacted by the noise in the channel and its messages are to be encoded in an optimal way.

Interestingly, such implications raise important research questions. For example, if a message encoding is essential to the process of transmission, then *what is the optimal encoding scheme?* If we go backwards and start from a digital data module, then the optimal scheme is the one that allows for an efficient and effective encoding/decoding of digital data. But, if we

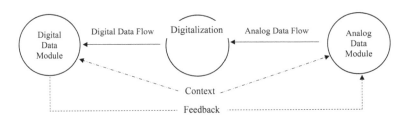

FIGURE 10.1
Digitalization within its context.

start where we really should start – at the analog data module, then finding an optimal scheme becomes a challenge. For example, if a listener Jim wants to hear a (digital) recording of a live rock concert, then who determines *what is noise and what is music* and what criteria does one use? If a buyer Mary wants to purchase a pair of nice fitting trendy jeans, then what are the aspects of the real thing that could be digitized and send to her for an appraisal?

This leads us to the point that in order to properly construct an appropriate encoding scheme we need to know the *relatively important dimensions*, which is a set of the criteria that *must be captured* by the encoding scheme. The main guiding principle, we suggest, is that of significance of the selected set of criteria to the context. In the cases of Jim and Mary we need to be able to figure out what is significant for them. Meaning, we must know what is significant for Jim to hear in live recording – what are the aspects that differentiate live vs. live audience recordings, and, in the case of Mary, we must know what attributes are applicable to adequately describe such term as "nice fitting trendy jeans".

Relative to the problem of defining the meaning of the term (which, fundamentally, involves comprising a string of words together and fixing the denotation by fiat), the problem of assessing the significance of a term is much larger and more complex. At this point we can put forward the following assertion:

Identification of the significance/impact of the construct is dependent on:

1. Knowledge of the mechanism of the impact, and
2. Identification of the context of the impact.

Let us discuss the requirements for determining the significance in order – we do so in the next chapter.

READER NOTES

Main points of agreement	
Supporting arguments (why agree?)	
Main points of disagreement	
Supporting arguments (why disagree?)	
Illustrative scenarios	
Possible research problem	
Possible research questions	

11

Mechanism of the Impact – What Is the Theory?

Let us summarize a current state of knowledge regarding the impact of digitalization, by prefacing it with a compilation of a list of knowns:

1. Digitalization *per se* is of no use, but its application for a given purpose makes it useful.
2. The intendent impact of digitalization is associated with the increases in efficiency and effectiveness of a target business process.
3. The impact of digitalization goes beyond the impact on the business process, where it also impacts the environment of the system that can be modeled by the business process.
4. The impact of digitalization goes beyond the impact on the business processes and the system, where it also impacts the context served by digitalization.

And we can stop right there, because at this point we have identified three levels of the impact (e.g., business process, system, context of the system) of digitalization.

So, let us start our consideration of the mechanism of the impact at the level of business process, which is intended to become more effective and efficient via digitalization. First, we need to go beyond the value that is provided by the process of conversion of analog data into digital data, because, again, it is not useful on its own. Let us consider if we can develop a suitable model of the impact – but this would require us to select an appropriate meta-model suitable for a theory. This is not to be confused with the perspective on digitalization as a complex system – this is a meta-model of the complex system itself. Here we concerned with the meta-model in the sense of a language that could be used to describe how the

DOI: 10.1201/9781003304906-11

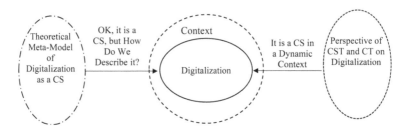

FIGURE 11.1
Meta-model and perspective on digitalization.

system works and why it works the way it does within its environment (see Figure 11.1).

So, one perspective deals with *what the system is,* and according to that perspective digitalization is a complex system that could be studied through the lens of Complex Systems Theory, and which could behave in certain ways, according to Chaos Theory. But, we also had an option of viewing digitalization as a mechanism, or an organism, or an economic model.

A theoretical meta-model, however, deals with how to *approach describing the system in its context.* For example, while we can use a perspective of complex systems to describe a human being as an instance of such system, we can use a variety of meta-models to guide the development of a description of a human being – we can do so using words, or mathematical equations, or images, or sounds, or chemical elements, and so on.

For purely illustrative purposes let us recall how a perspective and a meta-model go together, and we will use the example of Sir Isaac Newton and his take on what the Universe is that he outlined in his *Principia*:

> *Perspective – Mechanistic*: The Universe is a machine (a clock).
>
> *Meta-model – Judeo-Christian Theology*: Everything is created by God to do his work.
>
> *Synthesis*: The Universe is a machine created by God to do his work.

CONSIDERATION OF AN APPROPRIATE META-MODEL OF THEORY OF DIGITALIZATION

Regarding *knowledge of the mechanism of the impact* – in most of the fields of human endeavor supported by methods of scientific inquiry, this knowledge is supplied by theories via testing corresponding hypotheses. The process is straightforward, where the investigator:

- Selects a suitable for the purpose theory,
- Puts together a research model that is consistent with the theory, then
- Generates model-appropriate research questions, and
- Proceeds to operationalize the questions in the form of testable hypothesis, while not forgetting to
- State the acceptance/rejection criteria, and
- Goes ahead and tests the hypotheses.

It is important to note that the knowledge of the mechanism of the impact does not mean the *knowledge and understanding of how the mechanism actually works* in the sense of "*how X is causing Y*", but, rather, the meaning is in the simple sense of "*if X, then Y*". For example, why we can say, simplistically, "if human brain, then consciousness", and to proceed to successfully test such hypothesis, it would not imply that we know and understand, currently, how human consciousness comes into existence.

Fundamentally, one of the rewards for rejecting a null hypothesis comes in the form of the support for a prediction of the impact. If our testing supported that "if X, then Y" at time point of T_1, then, *ceteris paribus* and keeping in mind that science does not do well with absolute novelty, we have a reason to hypothesize that at time point T_2 the relationship "if X, then Y" would also hold.

Theories in current circulation may not always work, but, usually, they never completely fail. This is because if they do, we discard them and we aim for creating their replacements – new theories. An interesting case is when we do not have a theory allowing for predicting the impact of X on Y. And if this is the case, then we, literally, have nothing to go on, and the question becomes *What sort of a theory we may put forward and how do we go about putting one forward*?

To our knowledge, there is no *Theory of Digitalization* – there is no explanatory model of the mechanism by which digitalization produces its impact. And this is not surprising – after all, and at this point we do not:

- Have an established rigorous definition of what digitalization is
- Know, and did not define, what the outcomes of digitalization supposed to be

- Know, and did not specify, the context within which digitalization supposed to operate
- Know the outcome that digitalization supposed to produce within the context – all theories are context-specific.

So, at this point we are very far from being in a good position to predict *what this thing is going to do and how it is going to do it*. But, if we are to consider that digitalization is here to stay, and it is going to have its mechanism, and it is going to do something, then we also should consider having a theory for that. Consequently, we invite our reader to consider our attempt in suggesting what *sort of a theory* it *could* be – what sort of a meta-model could support *Theory of Digitalization*. We start by considering the most established models for theories that philosophers proposed – *syntactic, semantic*, and *pragmatic*. We also consider additional three perspectives on theory building, namely, *paradigmatic, third-world*, and *cognitive* models. In order to consider our options, we briefly introduce each theoretical model (TM#) first, and then we consider the fit of the model (FTM#) to the subject of interest of this paper – digitalization.

TM1: Syntactic Model

According to *syntactic* model (see works of Hempel, Nagel, Suppe for details), a theory must take a form of a universal generalization expressed in some sort of a formal language (e.g., predicate calculus). Within syntactic model it is a selection of *the language of the expression of generalizations* that is of fundamental importance to creating and formulating new theories. As a result, the question of utmost importance to semantic model is *What is the appropriate language for expressing a theory?*

FTM1: Applying syntactic structure to form *Theory of Digitalization* may seem an attractive proposition, for it would result in such statements as:

$$\left(Digital\ System\ Capacity, Digital\ System\ Staff\ Efficiency \right) \rightarrow$$
$$\left(Acquired\ Share\ New\ Business \right).$$

However, there are some issues that make syntactic model to be problematic for the purpose:

1. It relies on the assumption that a theory is logically deduced from universal generalizations, but it is problematic to generate such deductive explanations in such socio-technical domain as IS/IT.
2. It relies on universality of a causal structure embedded in a theory, but in a socio-technical domain there are many interrelated factors, some known and some unknown – this context makes a requirement of universality hard to achieve.
3. It does not characterize causality well – a statement "if X, then Y" within syntactic model does not allow for distinguishing between "increase in X *caused* increase in Y" and "increase in X *coincided with* increase in Y".
4. It does not suggest any ways for developing a theory – it is not clear on what basis we are to develop relevant to *Theory of Digitalization* hypotheses, or how do we use them to achieve relevant to digitalization goals.

TM2: Semantic Model

The aim of semantic model was to overcome "linguistic" (e.g., what language to use?) shortcomings of syntactic model by presenting a theory as a specification via a *proper model* (or *models*) of the universe of discourse. Hence, the major question raised by semantic model is *What is the appropriate model of the world that could serve as a basis for the theory?*

FTM2: Applying semantic model for the purposes of theory building has its benefits – for one, it is not language-dependent. Additionally, we humans do have a natural affinity for employing mental models and constructs, even if they are vaguely described – "Great job", "Good person", "Excellent health", and so one. However, this model also presents some issues:

1. While semantic model may feel at home within a domain of set theory, it is very difficult to apply to a socio-technical domain. This is because the *Universe of Discourse (UoD)* of digitalization is hard-to-impossible to formalize (e.g., the best we can do is to say that digitalization is a complex dynamic non-linear system, and so it is its context). But, a proper formalization in the form of a model is a fundamental requirement of a semantic model.

2. Even in the presence of a formalized model, semantic approach does not elaborate on the nature of the relationship between the constructs in the model. For example, given semantic model-based theory we may end up with such formalization as "(A, B, C, D)" – but semantic model does not offer any insights into:

   i. where the constructs (e.g., A, B, C, D) came from,

   ii. how to discover new ones, or

   iii. if there is a causal relationship between any of the constructs (e.g., A→C).

3. A proper formalization of UoD, based on semantic model, is the end in itself – semantic approach is not concerned with the nature of explanation. Consequently, if we apply semantic structure to form *Theory of Digitalization*, then we may end up with a good *representation* of UoD, but we'll have to go elsewhere if we are interested in an explanatory aspect of the formalized representation.

TM3: Pragmatic Model

Pragmatic perspective embraces the complexity of scientific theories, rejecting the idea that a theory could be expressed by a single linguistic construct or by a, however meaningful, formalized model. Instead, according to this view, syntactic structure of a theory and a meaning of a theory, while important, are secondary to the perspective that a true theory is a very complex representation, or amalgamation, of multiple sentences, perspectives, models, exemplars, and practices. *What makes a good person?* – this is a type of a problem that lends itself to be a subject of pragmatic model (however, in a well-specified context). Consequently, a theory should not be a discipline-specific, but, rather, it needs to be an inter-disciplinary construct, because a single perspective favored by a given field is necessarily limiting. Not surprisingly, the main question for pragmatic view is *What theoretical components, perspectives, and modes of theory-building are available in scientific theories across disciplines?*

FTM3: Applying pragmatic model for the purposes of theory building may seem attractive – it is not language-dependent, nor it is restrictive to a single perspective or a model. Undoubtedly, a theory crafted in accordance with pragmatic model would be truly multidimensional.

However, application of this perspective is problematic due to the following issues:

1. The complexity of socio-technical domain (e.g., digitalization) lends itself well to be dissected by a wide variety of disciplines, but it is not clear what models, perspectives and practices may work well across disciplines – it is difficult and not clear to decide what to keep and what to discard.
2. In order to be true to pragmatic model, which is strongly insistent on external and internal pluralism of theories, it is more appropriate to talk about *Theories of Digitalization*, where each theory is characterized by its own set of structures.
3. According to pragmatic model, structure of a theory is not isolated to scientific domain. Instead, it is an extension of and it is continuous with area of application of the theory – practice. From first glance, it is an attractive feature of pragmatic approach that allows for bridging rigor vs. relevance divide. Practically, however, the requisite complexity of such theory makes even meta-conceptualization a problematic undertaking – we would have to start considering all the relevant disciplines and areas that impact and are impacted by digitalization.

TM4: Paradigmatic Model

Paradigmatic model (see works of Kuhn) can be described as an attempt that straddles the gap between semantic model and pragmatic view on theory building. Based on this perspective, a theory could be modeled based on the appropriate *paradigm* – which could be expressed (again, according to Kuhn) as a *world view* or as a *set of exemplars*. This model takes much broader (and somewhat vaguer) view on theory building then semantic model does, but a much narrower perspective than one demanded by pragmatic model. This is because while a scientific paradigm required for theory building is a much larger construct than any single model of semantic view, it is incomparably smaller than a compilation of perspectives, models, exemplars, and practices coming from different fields that is required by pragmatic perspective.

Consequently, according to paradigmatic model the main question is *What is the appropriate perspective on the basis of which a model could be created?*

FTM4: Applying paradigmatic model for the purposes of theory building is an attractive proposition, because, it is safe to say, some scientific fields have a current and a prevalent paradigm of the field, or, a small set of competing paradigms. If this is the case, then all one needs to do is to follow a two-step process: first, select a fitting for the purpose paradigm, and, second, use the selected view as a basis for a new theoretical model. But, paradigmatic model is not a very suitable choice for our purposes due to the following reasons:

1. A *paradigm* is defined as a *world view* or a *set of exemplars* – it is not clear how such definitions could be applicable to the field of IS, or to a subject of digitalization, especially for the purposes of theory building. It is fair to say that, at this point, we do not have a common paradigm of the field, and it is a major undertaking to even consider synthesizing one. For example, we cannot accept such world view as "digital", because it is too limiting in scope (e.g., only works at the level of a basic, primarily binary, representation), and we cannot use something like *Technology Acceptance Model* as a foundation for a set of exemplars, exactly for the same reason.
2. This model may lend itself well in the case of the scientific fields with established world views or exemplars, but it is not clear how to construct a theory on the basis of the *emerging* world view or *still developing* exemplars. Simply put, a lot of things brought about and impacted by digitalization are going to be "new things", and paradigmatic model does not deal well with "new things".
3. Finally, paradigmatic model does not offer any suggestions regarding the process of discovering a *world view* or a *set of exemplars* within the field, nor does it offer any evaluation criteria on the basis of which the quality of the selected paradigm could be assessed.

TM5: Third World Model

Third world model (see works of Popper for details) bases a theory on the *world of objective contents of thought*, which is as real of a foundation as the first *world of physical objects or physical states*, or as the second world of states of consciousness or mental states (again, Popper). This is a very attractive view to take on the process of theory building, for this third world is the man-made universe comprised of a variety of constructs of thought, including theories and various logical relationships. But it is to be stressed that this world exists to a large extent independently. Resultantly, according to third world model the main question is *What is the best theory to select from the set, and once we do, then how do we formalize it?*

FTM5: Applying third world model for the purposes of theory building seems like a winning choice, because there is bunch of man-made, yet "objective" (e.g., objectively, universally, accepted) theories floating around and all we need to do is to pick a good one. However, there are problematic aspects that make this view doubtful to succeed for our purpose:

1. Modern cognitive science denies the major assumption of this view regarding the separation of states – worlds. For example, while this model espouses the distinction between first world of physical objects and events and second world of mental states, the current medical knowledge refutes it via evidence that *mental states are physical states of the brain.*

2. Approach to theories as being abstract entities residing within their autonomous universe offers no guidance regarding the process of discovering them, nor it offers any suggestions regarding the evaluation criteria that could be applied to the discovered theory.

3. If we are interested in causal relationships being a part of a theory, then this model offers no insights regarding such relationships, and if a question *Why X causes Y?* is asked, then we are bound to respond *Well, it simply does,* because we have nothing else to go on.

4. The issue of complexity of a construct and multidimensionality of the context further complicate an attempt to putting this view to use – the model offers no suggestions regarding the scope of theories, nor it suggests ways for reconciliation with competing theories, even if such are identified.

TM6: Cognitive Model

According to cognitive model a *theory is a mental representation of a functioning system* – this could be a mechanism, an organism, or a social system, where a mental representation is a mind/brain construct that stands for something (just like in linguistic view a word stands for something). One of the definition of *cognitive science*, the foundation of cognitive model, is as *the scientific study of the human mind. It is a highly interdisciplinary field, combining ideas and methods from psychology, computer science, linguistics, philosophy, and neuroscience. The broad goal of cognitive science is to characterize the nature of human knowledge – its forms and content – and how that knowledge is used, processed, and acquired.*[1] Based on this definition, we already may find it attractive for two simple reasons:

1. Aristotelian-based and mechanistic concept of *thinking as computation*, expressed in the form of computer science, is a part of the field of cognitive science, and computer science is instrumental to our subject – digitalization.
2. Cognitive science is explicitly multi-disciplinary, and digitalization, as a subject, is also multi-disciplinary.

According to cognitive model, a theory is a compilation of mental representations, where their main processes (such as exploration, explanation, assessment) are assessable via computation. In this regard, this view is consistent with mechanistic perspective on human cognition – it assumes, unlike romantic perspective, that thinking is computational in nature. This aspect is very important, for this view allows for evaluating competing theories *vis-à-vis* each other via explicit computational process. Naturally, according to cognitive model the main question is *What is the best mental representation of the (causal) relationships within the system?*

FTM6: Using cognitive perspective to theory building seems like a winning proposition, especially in comparison with abovementioned five other models. This is because, it would appear, that this approach allows for combining the benefits offered by syntactic and semantic views, while allowing for integrating both with paradigmatic perspective, with the added benefit that the resultant mental representation (paradigm in the sense of cognitive model) is multi-disciplinary and dissectible by means of computational analysis. The serious issue to address, of course, is of scope of the mental representation that is to serve as antecedent for a new theory. Specifically, the following points must be addressed:

1. How to scope the problem at hand and the corresponding mental representation?
2. How to select an appropriate set of tools – disciplines – to express the cognitive model?

3. How to, in the case of complex phenomena and in the absence of simple one-step causality in the sense of "if X, then Y", select the best causal chain spanning multiple constructs?

However, those are addressable questions, and one gets a sense that the answers to them could be obtained, and further refined, as the process of theory construction unfolds. We will illustrate to our reader, later in this book, how cognitive conception of theories could be applied for the purposes of creating a prototype of *Theory of Digitalization*.

However, there are no theories that are context-independent. Instead, theories are context-relevant and, as a result, we need to discuss the issue of the context of digitalization first. We will do so in the next few chapters.

NOTE

1. https://bcs.mit.edu/research/cognitive-science

READER NOTES

Main points of agreement	
Supporting arguments (why agree?)	
Main points of disagreement	
Supporting arguments (why disagree?)	
Illustrative scenarios	
Possible research problem	
Possible research questions	

12

Identifying the Context of Digitalization

The context of digitalization is represented by the *actors* who, one way or another, benefit from the existence of the system via a value that it provides. The actors could be actual human beings or they can be constructs implemented via technical system on behalf of humans, but regardless of their nature, they play certain *roles*, which take advantage of the use cases appropriate to the role of an actor.

In our consideration of the context of digitalization we can identify two basic roles. The first role is that of a *digital consumer* – an entity interested in utilizing digitalization for the purposes of reducing transaction costs. The second role is that of a *digital activist* – an entity interested in circulating information within a digital domain for the purposes of advancement of an agenda.

The suggested two-roles taxonomy relies on the following definitions:

- *A digital consumer is an actor who participates in transactions to acquire goods and/or services.*
- *A digital activist is an actor who promotes a particular idea or campaigns to bring about cultural, political or social change.*

Any actor with an access to a digital domain plays one or both roles, where a person could use digitalization as a digital consumer to purchase an item on-line, and then transition to the role of a digital activist to promote his agenda and to disseminate a message of some sort – even a message about the product or a vendor that sold it.

It is, probably, worth noting that this representation is different from, let us say, a representation provided by Use Case Diagram of UML, where a single actor could have an access to two different use cases – "Consumer Services" and "Activist Services" (see Figure 12.1). Instead, the suggested

DOI: 10.1201/9781003304906-12

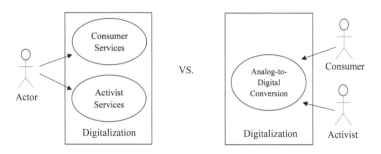

FIGURE 12.1
Different representations of digitalization.

representation emphasizes the role of an actor in the purpose-driven behavior of the system, where a single use case – "Digitization of Analog Data" could be used differently based on the intent of the actor.

This is because, fundamentally, the system of digitalization lacks intentionality and awareness – it "knows nothing" about what is done with its services – an actor could use her eBay digital platform, which is geared towards digital consumers, for the purposes of activism. And, similarly, an actor could use a social network to advertise or sell her goods and services to other participants. An illustration is provided by a usage of a vehicle by a driver – in one case a person may use his/her car as a purely utilitarian object that allows for moving cargo from point A to point B, and in another case the same car may serve as a source of entertainment – let us say, a person takes his car to a race track to drive fast and have some fun. But, regardless of the purpose, the car knows nothing about the intent of the driver. This may appear to be a minor point, but in our opinion it is a point worth making, for it allocates the proverbial blame to an intentionality of human agency and not to technology.

DIGITALIZATION: DIGITAL CONSUMERS

A group represented by *digital consumers* is primarily interested in using digitalization for the purposes of acquiring products and/or services on a marketplace, where they value efficiency and effectiveness of transactions that leads to a cost reduction associated with the purchase. Private citizens, social groups, large and small businesses – they all qualify as *digital consumers* as long as they employ digitalization as a tool of commerce in order to obtain an increase in received value and to decrease the associated cost of doing business. By interacting with digitalization, digital consumers acquire a *platform* allowing for purchasing products or services. The primary goal of obtaining a platform is to acquire a desired product/service, while a feedback to a product/service provider being a secondary activity. For all intents and purposes:

> Digital consumers are driven by the goal of minimization of transaction costs.

A sub-role that a *digital consumer* may play is that of a *digital vendor* – a consumer of digitalization that receives a tangible or intangible benefit from providing digitalization-based services to other digital consumers. Let us consider a scenario of an on-line Retailer A selling its items "direct to consumer" – from a perspective of digitalization, there are two digital consumers – Retailer A selling its wares and Customer B buying what is sold. Both parties derive benefits from using digitalization. Now, let us suppose we have a Firm C that is in charge of maintaining the site, or e-commerce suite, allowing for such scenario to take place. In this scenario Retailer A and Customer B are *digital consumers* of digitalization, where both parties aim to minimize transaction cost of an acquisition of a resource – Retailer A aims to acquire money of Customer B, and Customer B aims to acquire products of Retailer A. In such scenario Firm C is a *vendor* of digitalization, for it sells services allowing for minimization of the transaction costs to Retailer A and Customer B. Given a scenario of a buyer, a seller, and eBay marketplace, the buyer and seller are digital consumers and eBay is a vendor.

DIGITALIZATION: DIGITAL ACTIVISTS

The second group, *digital activists*, is represented by private citizens, groups, organizations and businesses that have a purpose of advancing an agenda. Consequently:

> Digital activists are driven by the purposes of introducing, propagating, and advancing a socio-political message directed towards changing a current status quo.

Activist must have, therefore, a program of some sort, but this does not mean that the program must be rational, realistic, or even beneficial to anyone outside of the given group of activists who subscribe to the program. By engaging digitalization, digital activists acquire a platform allowing for distributing information containing a message, where the primary goal is a dissemination of information, while receiving a feedback from recipients being is a secondary goal. While it is possible that some digital activists operate in a broadcast mode, where there is no feedback received from the intended audience, it is safe to say that most of the digital activists operate in duplex mode allowing for an audience feedback, and, consequently, for a fine-tuning of the message, which is important because it allows for a fine-tuning of the content and format of the distributed information.

It is worth noting that digital activists do not have to be the authors of a propagated message. For example, Jim uses his social network to propagate a message "Cole for Sheriff", where John may like the idea of Cole being a sheriff, and forwarding, and, thus, amplifying, the original message to his friends. Jennifer, on the other hand, does not like the idea of having Cole as a sheriff, and she offers a negative comment, or does not respond at all, of even blocks the messages containing "Cole for Sheriff" or, going even further, blocks Jim. All three actors in this case utilize digitalization as digital activists. We can call Jim, who sent out the message, a *message generator*. John, who re-sent the message with the intent of increasing its impact, a *message advocate/amplifier*. Jennifer, on the other hand, did not like the message and wanted its impact to be minimized – Jennifer is a *message suppressor*.

However, Jennifer could respond differently – she could start her own stream of messages (e.g., "Cole is a Loser – Do Not Vote Cole for Sheriff!") that aim to counter the message generated by Jim. If this is the case, then Jennifer becomes a message generator. It is probably safe to say that the majority of generated by digital activists' messages are *against some other message* – in the case of Jim, the message could be presented as "Cole is a better candidate than others to run for Sheriff", and in the case of Jennifer the content of the message could be "Any other candidate is better than Cole to run for Sheriff".

But what about a situation where Carl is very active in posting messages related to his athletic activities on his social network, the same place where Mary is posting her pictures from her garden? Clearly, Carl and Mary are digital activists that disseminate messages promoting themselves, where the basic message is "The People of the World Are Better Off Knowing

About Me!" or "I Have the Information That You Need!" The unfortunate part, however, that there is no peer review – the hypothetical value that is delivered to others via the content of such message is completely based on the subjective appraisal of a message generator.

READER NOTES

Main points of agreement	
Supporting arguments (why agree?)	
Main points of disagreement	
Supporting arguments (why disagree?)	
Illustrative scenarios	
Possible research problem	
Possible research questions	

13

Digitalization: Platform Acquisition

The suggested categorization of the actors based on *digital consumers* and *digital activists* could be perceived as simplistic. But, nevertheless, it is useful and it is based on a differentiation between *what kind of a platform is being acquired as a result of using digitalization* – making a distinction between transactions involving a *message* and transactions dealing with an acquisition or a sale of a *product or a service*. It is important to note that we do not take into consideration any issues associated with the *rationality* of the decision-making process of the involved actor, or the *relative value* of what is being acquired. Instead, we simply base our categorization on *what is being acquired by an actor via digitalization.*

Consequently, we assume the same degree of rationality of a decision maker when she is acting within an analog domain or a digital domain (e.g., digitalization does not impact rationality). Similarly, we also assume that the perceived value of a product remains the same regardless of whether the access to the product is via analog or digital channel (e.g., digitalization does not make a product *itself* more valuable). What adds value, however, is an information channel used to deliver a message or a product. This is similar to a perception that two identical gift items differ in their value because of the difference in wrapping paper.

Under such taxonomy of the roles, we provide the following differentiation:

- *Digital consumers are the actors who utilize digitalization to acquire a platform for purchasing products or services, while*
- *Digital activists are the actors who utilize digitalization to acquire a communication platform.*

DOI: 10.1201/9781003304906-13

In the case of digital consumers and digital activists alike, the *general expectations* of digitalization are the same, namely, both types of digital actors expect improvements in *efficiency and effectiveness of the interface provided by the resultant platform*. Both roles are driven by maximization of the expected value received via digitalization.

An important point of note is that *the acquisition of a digital platform is not the end of the process* – quite the opposite, it is just a beginning, for it is a point of entry into a digital domain. This is because digital consumers and digital activists alike are offered an opportunity for a *platform upgrade*, the purpose of which is to assure the persistence of the users within the digital domain – to make the first-time and occasional users into regular users. As for the regular users, the action coming from digitalization would be geared towards creating some sort of a logical hierarchy of importance – establishing a ranking among the users (e.g., a system of ratings of the users, moderators, and so on comes to mind).

For example, digital consumers could become preferred customers, where they get the first dibs on promotions, exclusive events, special pricing, and so on. In a similar fashion, digital activists are offered paths to becoming moderators, chat administrators, senior members, and so on, where they can monitor messages of others, but also are given an opportunity to emphasize and promote preferred information and de-emphasize and restrict the dissemination of the "unaligned" information.

However, digital consumers and digital activists assign a different *meaning* to the value provided by digitalization, because they have a different interpretation of what *improvements* delivered via digitalization mean. Consequently, it is fair to say that the *manifestation of the expectation* is different for two roles – *the expectation of the value of digitalization is role-dependent*. The difference stems from the difference in the target outcome, where:

- *Digital consumers aim to minimize the resources they spend on the acquisition of the product or service.* Here, our assumption is that the digital consumers use digitalization in order to acquire a desired product/service at, *ceteris paribus*, cheapest price with the least amount of resources (e.g., time, energy spent on search). Thus,

Digital consumers are driven by the goal of acquisition of resources.

Digital consumers of digitalization who are producers, distributors, or sellers of goods and services are driven by acquisition of monetary resources of their customers. On the other hand, digital consumers who are purchasers of goods and services are driven by the acquisition of those goods and services.

- *Digital activists aim to maximize the reach (e.g., intensity, width and strength of the distribution) of their message.* In the case of this scenario, our assumption is that an activist uses digitalization to make her message known to as large of an audience, as it is desired by the actor or as it is feasible given her state within the system of digitalization. Consequently,

Digital activists are driven by the goal of dissemination of their messages.

One of the potential problems for digital activists is the presupposition that from the very beginning the context for disseminating of the messages is expected to be disproportionally large relative to the available analog context. This carries an important implication – while digital consumers do not expect transaction costs to be reduced to zero, or to become negative (e.g., a scenario where digital consumers do not pay, but, instead, get paid for their purchases), digital activists do not have an expectation of reaching the limit of the context of their message. Meaning, if "digitalization-consumer" interactions are "bound to terminate", then "digitalization-activist" interactions are not – they are self-perpetuating for there is no termination point when digital activist can say "OK, we got our message out and we are done".

Consequently, effectiveness and efficiency of digitalization is perceived by digital consumers as a *degree of minimization of interactions* associated with the purchase of a product/service, while it is perceived by digital activists as a *degree of maximization of the exposure* of their message.

It is worth noting that digital consumers will stop using digitalization when the end result (e.g. acquisition of a product/service) is achieved or if the benefits are not, or no longer, feasible to obtain (e.g., the transaction costs are not decreased). For example, if Bob cannot renew his driver's license on-line, and he cannot schedule an appointment to do so on-line, then Bob would, eventually, decide to go to the office and to renew his license in-person. Digital activists, on the other hand, have no incentives to stop using digitalization, because the quest for maximization of the exposure of the message is almost boundless.

The expected corollary is that:

> Expected outcomes of digitalization differ depending on the role played by a given actor, because different roles are associated with different expectations.

For example, a maker of baseball bats, Louisville Slugger, may manufacture its product according to the precise specifications and by following a strict process allowing for producing a great *output*. However, the *outcome* of manufacturing a baseball bat will be only superficially defined by whether or not the product is purchased. On a deeper level, the outcome is, of course, whether or not the product satisfies the customers' needs or wants. And those, in our example, would differ depending on whether it is used by a baseball player to hit a baseball or by a gangster to threaten his victim.

We can consider, as another example, an instance of digitalization adopted by Excellent University in order to offer an on-line degree geared towards the entry of the graduates into a workforce. We can depict the overall process of education of on-line students by using three components – input, output, and input/output production process. In the case of Excellent University, the *inputs* are in the form of incoming freshmen, the process of input-output production is the digitalized on-line education process, and the *outputs* represented by graduating students. What we can call a *surface-level outcome* of digitalization is whether or not a graduating student Jane gets a job offer. But the *base-level outcome* is more important – it is whether Business X (a potential employee of Jane) is satisfied with the education she received. This is because if Business X is satisfied, then it will continue (given the need) hiring graduates of Excellent University. Additionally, it validates the product offered by Excellent University. But, clearly, the picture may be different if Excellent University aims to offer its new on-line degree to prepare the students for pursuing a different set of goals.

READER NOTES

Main points of agreement	
Supporting arguments (why agree?)	
Main points of disagreement	
Supporting arguments (why disagree?)	
Illustrative scenarios	
Possible research problem	
Possible research questions	

14

Digitalization: Outcomes of Using a Platform

At this point we can consider typical illustrative scenarios of the *impact of the roles on determining outcomes* in the context of digitalization. Based on our taxonomy of *digital consumers* vs. *digital activists*, if Mary Jane is buying an aviation headset on-line, then she is *purchasing a product*, which makes her a *digital consumer* who purchased a platform, or instantiated digitalization, to complete an economic transaction. Conversely, if Mary Jane is posting a content proclaiming her affinity for a politician advocating for a particular set of policies, then, by means of using digitalization, she is *purchasing a platform for communicating a message*, which makes her a *digital activist*.

We acknowledge that there are areas where a message may be tightly coupled with a product, as in the case where a purchased product is symbolic of an idea. For example, a person buying a hybrid or electric car *could* be seen as a consumer making a choice on a basis of a set of utilitarian criteria as they apply to a product. Conversely, this consumer could also be seen as a carrier of a socio-political message that is associated with the car. Same applies to a situation when a person is buying a coffee at a "fair trade" store – this could be because the person likes the coffee, or because the person feels that she is making an important socio-political statement.

But, a large sub-set of such situations is fairly straightforward to deal with. If Person A purchases a sweatshirt with a "Support NRA" logo, and a Person B purchases a t-shirt with a logo that says "Guns Kill", then we can convincingly conclude that they have done so not by acting as digital consumers, but as digital activists. The situation with *digital vendors* is fairly straightforward as well – vendor acts as an interface allowing for instantiating digitalization by digital consumers and digital activists. As a

DOI: 10.1201/9781003304906-14

result, vendors sell access to the digital platform provided by digitalization to digital consumers and digital activists.

It is, probably, fair to say that under such categorization vendors are neither interested in products or services purchased by digital consumers, nor they are necessarily moved by the messages and ideas of activist. It is obviously possible that given a diverse and decentralized inventory of used vehicles car aficionados may create and maintain a website for purchasing, selling, and trading in used cars, however, it is clearly not a requirement. Similarly, a group of digital activists may select a social network to conduct its business and to communicate with general public regardless of their approval of the social network leadership regardless of their perspectives.

However, ideally, we would like to see vendors of digitalization as an unbiased and neutral interface between digital consumers or digital activists and digitalization. This is because any inclination or preference that vendors possess and display would impact the experience of digital consumers and digital activists (e.g., as an anti-conservative bias demonstrated by Facebook). Overall, the presence of vendors is a result of a natural desire of digital consumers and digital activists for the ease of access to digitalization. But, as we can see, such ease of access is paid for if not in terms of money, then in terms of the introduction of extra layer of complexity – this results in inevitable decrease in efficiency of transactions. Thus, it is reasonable to expect a movement to *vendor-free* or *vendor-less* platforms. Let us consider interactions that take place between digitalization, digital consumers, and digital activists (see Figure 14.1).

First, in regard to "Consumer-Digitalization" relationship – the affair is purely transactional, and the consumer interacts with digitalization by means of two information channels: "Request of a product" and "Receipt of the product". Under such circumstances, what is valued by a consumer is the extent of effectiveness and efficiency of the transaction as it is mediated by digitalization.

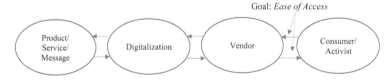

FIGURE 14.1
Interaction with digitalization.

Let us consider a simple equation reflecting a price of a product for a customer, where

$$Total\ Product\ Cost = Cost\ Of\ Product + Cost\ Of\ Transaction.$$

And a large portion of transaction cost associated with the purchase is the cost of using digitalization. This does not have to be expressed in terms of a monetary value, but could be reflected in terms of time, energy, or any other resource that a consumer has to spend getting the product. As a result, the cost of transaction is represented by a totality of interactions between the customer and digitalization, where more customer-digitalization interactions means higher cost of transactions. It is only natural to aim for minimizing the cost of transactions, thus, aiming for minimizing the number of interactions.

As a result, the goal of the successful interaction in "digital consumer-digitalization" scenario is to keep the number of communication sessions and exchanged messages to a minimum. This means that the optimal interaction is of the type "Ordered product" followed by "Received Product", and any additional communication may occur only in the case of exceptions – such as in the case of customer complains, delayed order inquiry regarding the status of a late delivery, additional questions, etc. Consequently, a normal progression of utilization of digitalization could be seen as two-pronged process – first, directed at elimination of vendors (e.g., Nike sells its sneakers directly from its factory, Tesla sells its cars directly to consumer), second, toward minimization of communication sessions associated with the purchase of products (e.g., printer running low on ink places an order for a refill without any involvement of a customer, software upgrades to a computer or a car without requiring any customer interaction).

Now, in regard to "digital activist-digitalization" relationship – the affair is more complex, and this is not because of the difference in output. Instead, the difference, is in the *general expectation of the result* from a transaction. In both cases the general expectation is maximization of value, but what differs is the manifestation of general expectations. While one customer may go to a store in order to get food she enjoys (e.g., to get as much pleasure out of food as possible), another person may go to the same place in order to get the best bang for a buck and to purchase as much food for as little money as possible.

In the case of digital consumers, it is expected that a digitalization-enabled transaction allows for getting the best available deal that is still reflective of a *fair value*. For example, by using Web-based resources a consumer may find an item that was discounted 90%, and proceed to purchase the item. In this case, this consumer found a great deal that is still *considered to be a fair deal by both parties* – by the consumer and by the business selling the item at 90% discount (because this is a better option than to get nothing). This implicit assumption of mutual fairness of value prevents a consumer from endlessly searching for items that are priced at zero dollars and ship free, of for items that the seller will pay for to a consumer to receive.

However, in the case of digital activists the *expectation of what is a fair value for instantiating and interacting with digitalization is oversize*. Let us consider, first, what digital activists provide as an input to digitalization. The answer is simple – it is a message of some sort that digital activists want to propagate. The target of the activist's message is a wider social group than that aligned with the views of an activist, for there is no point to actively propagate the message that is already accepted within the group that the activist is a part of. For example, there is not much benefit in using a web site of a church in order to advocate the parishioners to become the members of that church. Consequently, an activist would expect that digitalization would allow for reaching a wider audience for her message than otherwise possible. An interesting question to ask, however, is what is an appropriate digital context that is a larger then that within which the message is already accepted? Meaning, what would be an appropriate "super group" in a hypothetical hierarchy?

Digitalization fulfills this expectation of spreading a message outside the group by the means of *message amplification*, which is achieved by increasing the:

1. *Intended target audience for the message* – this allows for reaching a wider audience that otherwise possible.
2. *Frequency of the delivery of the message* to the target audience – this allows for sending messages to the audience more often than otherwise possible.
3. *Diversity of the formats of the message* – this allows for presenting the message in a greater variety of formats and forms than otherwise possible.
4. *Persistency of the message* – this allows for increasing the consistency of the presence of the message, which is achieved by increasing the exposure of the target audience to the more frequent messages in a variety of formats.

5. *Level of protection from a negative feedback* – this allows for a better allocation of resources dedicated to spreading the message, because an activist does not have to face the opposing audience unless the confrontation is desired.

Simply put, an activist would not consider an ability to send a single message to a designated group of people to be a fair value reward for using digitalization. Instead, a fair value (read, *surface-level outcome*) would be considered an ability to send a message:

1. To as large of a group of people as possible
2. In as many different formats as possible
3. As often as possible, while
4. Receiving as little of a negative feedback as possible

An important point to consider, then, is the intended boundary of the message. Let us say, Billy really likes the movie he saw last night. So, Billy decides that it is a good idea to let everyone know that the movie was good and everyone should watch it. What would be a reasonable expectation that Billy may have regarding the scope of the propagation of the message? What would be considered, in the case of an activist, a "sufficient level of exposure" for a given message that was disseminated? Is there a limit, where an activist would say: "OK, this is enough, the job is done..."? Or, is it possible that there is no limit at all? Let us consider a political candidate Bob that is, well, not liked by Sam – would Sam be satisfied if his message "Bob is not good!" would be propagated across his social network? Across networks? It is an interesting question to consider.

If we consider an interaction of an actor with digitalization, then we can portray it as two different schemes working in two different cases presented in Figure 14.2 and Table 14.1.

First, in the case of a consumer the interaction is a closed loop of "consumer→ digitalization→ consumer" and, second, in the case of an activist the interaction is a linear chain of "activist→ digitalization→ target audience". As a result, it is not hard to see why a consumer may want to minimize the interaction with digitalization, while an activist may aim to maximize it – while a consumer does have to pay the consequences for the interaction in the form of the expenditure of resources, an activist does not.

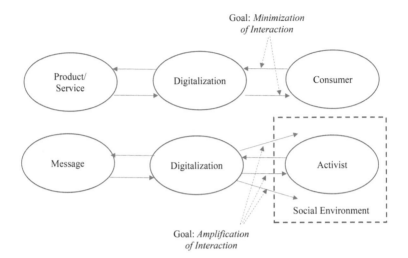

FIGURE 14.2
Role-specific goals of interaction with digitalization.

TABLE 14.1

Role-Specific Requirements for Interaction with Digitalization

Attribute	Digital Consumers	Digital Activists
Source	Consumer (self)	Activist (self)
Destination	Consumer (self)	Target audience (others)
Parties involved	Minimum audience	Maximum audience
Width of channel	As wide as necessary	As wide as possible
Frequency	As low as possible	As high as possible
Format	Minimization	Maximization
Persistency	Limited to the necessary interaction	Limited to the life span of the message

READER NOTES

Main points of agreement	
Supporting arguments (why agree?)	
Main points of disagreement	
Supporting arguments (why disagree?)	
Illustrative scenarios	
Possible research problem	
Possible research questions	

15

Identifying the Scope of the Environment

Thus far we identified two roles for the actors that *instantiate the system of digitalization* just as a driver instantiates "car driving" process. The next step, then, is to outline the boundary of what, actually, comprises the extent of the system of *digital consumers* and *digital activists* – we need to scope the context of digitalization. Let us look at the issue through the lens of CST. The first implication of this perspective is that a social group is open to its environment, impacts it, and is impacted by it. Consequently, it is difficult to correctly scope the context purely on the basis of the societal boundaries even within a well-defined territory (e.g., as it is in the case of *nation states*). It is also difficult to close the context on the basis of such attributes as a spoken language, religion, and so on.

Let us consider an illustrative example that helps differentiating *general context* and the *scope of the context*. Suppose, Billy is an expert in fixing lawn mowers and he regularly posts "how to fix a lawn mower" videos on YouTube. Billy's general context is represented by those people who watch YouTube videos (e.g., have a computer and an access to the Internet via a browser or a YouTube app). The scope of the Billy's context, however, is smaller and it is represented by a subset of the people who are interested in his videos.

In order to answer the question regarding the scope of the context of digitalization, we suggest using a set of the sub-questions and the corresponding general answers (see Table 15.1) based on the content of the previous chapters.

The answers to the questions provide a sufficient foundation for guiding a search for answering the question of a scope of a given context. For example, if Company X decides to invest in a new digitalization initiative,

TABLE 15.1

Investigating the Scope of the Context of Digitalization

Sub-Question	General Answer
What is the general context of digitalization?	The context could be defined via two roles – *digital activists* and *digital consumers*.
What is the outcome of digitalization?	The outcome is a delivery of a role-specific value – for a consumer it is a purchase of a product, and for an activist it is a dissemination of a message.
What forces of the environment digitalization must be able to counter?	Digitalization is under compressive and expansive forces of the environment, resulting in the continuous quest for gains in efficiency and effectiveness of the system.
Is there a gap between the output of digitalization and its outcome?	The inevitable gap is associated with the difference in value between a resource (e.g., digital data) and the utilization of the resource (e.g., reduced transaction cost)
What are the mechanisms and tools allowing for assessing the quality of the outcome?	The ways of assessing the quality of outcome are role-specific and ontologically subjective.
What are the costs associated with the provision of the outcome?	The ways of assessing the cost of the outcome is dependent on two factors: first, identifying the scope of the impact of digitalization, and, second, identifying a set of negative factors that must be addressed within the scope of the context.

then the overarching question would be *What value would it provide to its customers?* And the provided sub-questions and their general answers could help in answering the big question. However, as our reader can see, the general questions and their hypothetical answers become gradually more complex, where the addressing the question of the cost of the outcome of digitalization is the most difficult, conceptually and practically, to address.

Provided above general answers allow for considering the question of the context of digitalization – in order to do so we apply *synthesis* as a method of inquiry and proceed along the following three steps:

1. Identify the larger system that contains digitalization.
2. Understand the behavior and properties of the larger system.
3. Disaggregate the understanding of the containing system by understanding the functions of digitalization within the containing system.

Let us begin by stating a set of the following assumptions (*A#*):

A1: *Output* of digitalization is data/information in digital format

A2: *Impact* of digitalization is the increase in effectiveness and efficiency of delivery of the digital data/information

A3: *Outcome* of the digitalization is the generation of *value* as a result of the impact

A4: *Context* of digitalization is any environment that:

- Has an infrastructure to utilize it
- Has an audience that may utilize and benefit from the generated value

Finally, we state the important to the subject of this chapter assumption:

A5: *Context* of digitalization is a *socio-technical system.*

While *A5* seems to be a too obvious of a proposition, we feel that it is important to state it explicitly, because a context of digitalization *cannot be* represented by a purely technical environment. Similarly, *the context of digitalization cannot be a purely social system*, because in order to interface with digitalization its environment must have a digital interface. For example, a person cannot receive an e-mail without having a computer.

At this point we can propose a definition of the *general context* of digitalization, as follows:

A context of digitalization is a socio-technical environment (system) comprised of two interfacing components:

1. *Social component, which is represented by humans and the analog-to-analog interactions between them*
2. *Technical component, which is represented by:*
   - *Analog-to-digital interface (allowing for context-to-context interaction)*
   - *Digital-to-digital interface (allowing for context-to-digitalization interaction)*

Consequently, we can also propose a definition of the *scope of the context* of digitalization, as follows:

The scope of the context of digitalization is any socio-technical system that has the:

- *Technical infrastructure to interface with it and*
- *Social component that is willing to use it and derives a perceived value from its output.*

As we determined earlier, the two roles that such socio-technical system could play are those of a *digital consumer* and of a *digital activist.* It seems reasonable to conclude that the parties interested in expansion of digitalization would dedicate most of their attention to developing a socio-technical interface that allows the social component to be "sucked in" into the interactions with the technical component. An obvious example is a smart speaker taking voice commands, or a self-checkout relying on face recognition technology.

In the case of *digital consumers,* however, the scope of the context is determined by a *transaction,* because it is in the interest of consumers to keep the scope of the process of purchasing a product as small as possible. After all, one of the main goals of almost any consumer is to minimize transactions costs associated with purchases of goods and services. Intuitively, this would inevitably result in the situation where most of the increase in the scope of digitalization would come by means of commoditization of the services, via a simple increase in the number of transactions.

This brings us to the issue of finding other ways for increasing the scope of the context of digitalization. In order to do so we need to consider some of the ways by which digitalization may *grow,* or expand, and *develop,* or evolve. The aspect of growth of digitalization is the easiest one to deal with, for it will take place via expansion of A2D services provided by the system. This expansion, highly likely, will proceed along the two routes:

- By substituting and eliminating a human element that was previously responsible for the services. This can be exemplified by a scenario where an eBay seller decides to start printing shipping labels at home instead of going to the post office.
- By developing new areas suitable for application of A2D conversion services. For example, this could manifest in the form of developing a custom diet and personalized fitness program based on the suggestions from AI-based algorithms.

The aspect of development, or evolution, of digitalization is more interesting, but also is more complex because we don't have good illustrative examples at this point. But we could consider, for example, a range of scenarios where all of them involve transformative changes to A2D interface between the context and the digital representation of the context. At the simpler range of scenarios, we can start from a person being able to order new prescription glasses based on the reading of a digital scanner that eliminates the involvement (in most of the cases) of an optometrist. At the more complex level, we will encounter situations where digital systems impose, via the interface, a new discrete structure on a continuous analog reality of a context. A precursor of this is an example of purchasing a paint from a home improvement store, where a shopper encounters an abundance of digitized colors to select from. Under such scenario any custom color comes from a list of previously predefined set of colors.

Another example of the scenario for development, or evolution, of digitalization is as follows:

> Early in the morning, a bio sensor reads the data generated by the body of a sleeping digital consumer. The data is compiled and is sent away for processing. The resultant information is used to determine the current state of health of the person and the recommended daily supplements. This determination is used to select the vitamins and/or foods for the day. The order is sent to the pharmacy and/or grocery store, where it is filled automatically. Once the order is ready, it is delivered, without a human participation, to the consumer whose account is charged automatically. In the case if the consumer refuses to receive and take the prescribed foods and supplements, the notification to his health insurance is automatically send and the premiums are automatically recalculated. However, if within a short period of time the bio sensor identifies the changes in the body caused by the intended diet and medicine, then the confirmation is sent to the associated health insurance center, where it is processed and the corresponding message to the digital consumer is generated: "Good job today! You earned another 10 points toward your monthly discount towards things that are good for you!"

READER NOTES

Main points of agreement	
Supporting arguments (why agree?)	
Main points of disagreement	
Supporting arguments (why disagree?)	
Illustrative scenarios	
Possible research problem	
Possible research questions	

16

Identifying the Outcome of Digitalization

A consideration of the "perceived value" delivered by digitalization to its context brings our attention to a very important question – *What is the outcome of digitalization?*

It is clear that the *output* of digitalization is data/information in digital format, and it cannot be anything else due to the nature of the system. Consequently, *the value of the output* of digitalization – the outcome, could be derived from *what is done* with the generated digital data. In this regard we have two options – let us consider them in order.

> *Option 1: The generated digital data is intended to be utilized in "as is" state without further alterations, conversions and formatting.*

This case could be exemplified by a scenario where Mary records a conference presentation of Bob on her phone, so she can listen to it again at her convenience. In such case, Mary converts (via digitalization) the analog signals into digital format and it is the utilization of the data in digital format that serves as an outcome of digitalization. Here we have the following chain of links: "*analog/digital data→ digitalization→ digital data→ consumption of digital data*", where "*consumption of digital data*" is the outcome of digitalization that is going to generate value.

> *Option 2: The generated digital data is intended to be utilized in "to be" state resulting from additional alterations, conversions and formatting.*

As an illustrative example for this case we can consider the extension of the first scenario, where Jane ends up in possession of a digital recording

DOI: 10.1201/9781003304906-16

of Thomas' presentation. But let us suppose that Jane did not like the presentation of Thomas, and, by extension, she did not like Thomas – she disagrees with the political views and opinions of a presenter. Let us consider what digital format allows Jane to do with the recorded presentation:

1. Jane can use the original presentation to identify, select, and cut out the points that emphasize the differences in perspectives between her and the presenter – the selected content can be taken out of context and used to Jane's advantage to present Thomas in negative light.
2. The selected segments could be used as a narrative behind a video or an image portraying Thomas in a more negative way than he appeared during the presentation.
3. The selected points of disagreement could be played and re-played continuously to emphasize the differences and to crystallize the negative image of Thomas within the audience that is friendly to Jane.
4. Jane can convert the presentation to text, then apply dramatic formatting to the selected, taken out-of-context parts to portray Thomas in negative light.
5. Jane may disseminate, widely, all the mentioned above derivatives of the original presentation among the members of the audience she is intended on impacting.

Obviously, all the options mentioned above are available for the purposes of doing the opposite – namely, to emphasize the positive aspects instead of negative.

Consequently, what we get in the case of Option 2 is a not the original digital data outputted by digitalization, but a "digital Frankenstein" – a *purpose-oriented compilation of manipulated digital artefacts that bears little resemblance to the original.*

And if the second scenario is a viable one to consider, then digitalization *is not a content-neutral system.* Instead, it is a *content-manipulating system.* Digitalization impacts the content – data and information to be consumed by digital and analog audience, and it impacts the content very strongly. This is analogous to using a dough to make bread or to make crackers or croutons – the form of the end product impacts the content of the final product.

Let us consider two aspects of any message – there is a substance of the message, and there is a format of the message. The substance of the message is *a syntactically-correct semantic content to be interpreted by the intended audience,* and it is prepared in accordance with socio-cultural norms of the group for which the message was constructed or within which the message is to be interpreted. Let us suppose that a group of people wants you to vote for Joe Bob. In an analog/social domain such advocacy may take a form of a poster or a chant "Vote for Joe Bob!" The syntactic form and semantics of the message are clear – this is a call advocating to vote for a particular person, and it is very doubtful that an English-speaking person may misinterpret the meaning of the message. If taken from analog to digital domain, the semantic content of the message remains the same. The format of the message serves as *a packaging for the semantic content.* In general, any message, digital or analog, is characterized by a set of attributes provided in Table 16.1.

It is important to keep in mind that every message has a *cost of delivery* within the intended context. When the scope of the intended dissemination of information is narrow – let us say, Joe Bob lives in a small rural county, then the cost of delivery of analog messages is comparable to (or cheaper) the cost of delivery of digital messages advocating "Vote for Joe Bob!" But once the scope of the intended audience grows bigger, in terms of the geography and the size of the population, the cost of delivery of digital messages falls due to the scalability of digital infrastructure that counters the law of diminishing returns. However, the cost of delivery of analog messages rises – again, due to the same law of diminishing returns. Thus, digitalization offers a set of tangible advantages over its analog counterpart as it is illustrated in Table 16.2.

TABLE 16.1

Attributes of a Message

Attribute of a Message	Description of the Attribute
Persistence of the impact	Duration of time within which the message remains relevant (sign "Vote for Joe Bob" persists longer than the spoken phrase)
Timeframe of the impact	Period of time during which the message carries its intended meaning
Preferred format	The intended way of presentation of the content
Preferred medium	The intended medium for message communication
Intended audience	A sub-set of the population targeted by the content of the message
Channels of delivery	Transmission medium-specific mode of delivery of the message
Frequency of delivery	How often the intended audience should be exposed to the message

TABLE 16.2

Message-Related Advantages of Digitalization

Advantage of Digitalization	Source of Advantage
Lower cost of formatting a message	A given content can be presented in a nearly infinite number of formats, inexpensively (e.g., via templates)
Lower cost of inter-media conversion	A given message can be converted from one type of a medium to another, inexpensively (e.g., spoken word transcribed, text-to-speech conversion)
Lower cost of portability	Diversity of the audience for a message necessitates a variety of formats and media that carries the message – an almost infinite variety of forms of a message could be stored inexpensively
Lower cost of replicating the message	A large audience requires a large number of messages – it is inexpensive to create multiple copies of a message
Lower cost of demand planning	Digitalization allows for "real-time" response to the requirements of the context – it is easy and inexpensive to scale up or down
Lower cost of dissemination of the message	A single digital channel allows for a very effective and efficient dissemination of the messages, where a cost of delivery is decreasing with the increase in the number of messages
Lower cost of temporal persistence of the message	Presentation of a message in various formats via a variety of media is inexpensive, and this allows for creating a "message campaign" expanding the time frame within which the message is active
Lower cost of expanding the time frame of the impact of the message	A variety of inexpensive information channels, paired with a variety of inexpensive messages in different formats using different media, allows for easy dissemination of the messages

If this is the case, then we can consider that the expected by the actor's outcome of digitalization, the generated value, is associated with the ability to modify the original (e.g., analog) message using digital tools with the goal of increasing the impact of the message. The obvious question, then, is:

Whether a digitally modified message is a valid representation of the original one?

Let us consider a 3-D printer that is used to manufacture a plastic gun that is used in murder. We would be hard-pressed to equate the inputs – a plastic, with the output – the printed gun. Likely, we agree that the raw materials differ in *kind*, rather than in *degree*, from the product of the printing process. However, we do not have similarly easy way of separating original analog messages from digitally modified ones. Let us consider an illustrative example summarized in Table 16.3.

TABLE 16.3

Example of Advantages of Digitalization

Advantage of Digitalization	Example: Simple Text "Vote for Joe Bob!"
Lower cost of formatting a message	Application of a variety of fonts, font sizes, colors, backgrounds
Lower cost of inter-media conversion	Message can be converted, easily: • from text to audio (text-to-speech) • from text to image • from text to video
Lower cost of portability	Digital storage is cheap, and the movement of the stored data/messages is inexpensive – it is easy and cheap to send via the Internet a file/folder containing multiple forms of a message recorded in a variety of media
Lower cost of replicating the message	Scalability of replication allows for generating a desired number of copies based on the local demand
Lower cost of demand planning	Inexpensive storage, movement of the storage, and replication allow for meeting any changes in demand generated by the context
Lower cost of dissemination of the message	Digital messages lend themselves well to hyperlinked content easily accessible by the audience – "pull" format of dissemination. Digital messages are easy and cheap to disseminate and "push" on the audience. Digital messages are easy to disseminate via inter-audience communication – "audience push/pull", where a recipient can forward a message to other members of the audience
Lower cost of temporal persistence of the message	Digitized message, presented in a variety of formats and different media, could provide a higher degree of "information persistence" for the audience (e.g., you see a text, then you see an image, then you hear audio, then video, etc.)
Lower cost of expanding the time frame of the impact of the message	While some of the messages have a "deadline" (e.g., election), they don't have to have a point of a beginning – and the information campaign could be started much earlier if it is conducted in digital format. And earlier start contributes to early exposure, and to higher degree of familiarity with and acclamation to the message

At this point, we are warranted to put forward yet another proposition:

Digitalization is a system allowing for alteration of the interpretation of information by means of manipulating:

1. The format of the information
2. The frequency of delivery of information
3. The speed of delivery of information

This capability to impact the interpretation of a message is not unique to digitalization – any medium has it. A person could say "Help!" in many different ways, and the format of the message will impact the interpretation of the word. If we use a regular mail, then the interpretation of the content of the letter could be influenced by its envelope, the paper it is typed on, the font, the color, and so on.

In some scenarios, digitalization is used for the purposes of data conversion and consequent storage. This could be case of digitizing analog images and videos, or accounting records, or medical files, and so on. But, more often, digitalization is used for the purposes that go beyond those of simple data conversion and storage. And if we keep in mind that information is always used for a purposes of obtaining some sort of an impact, then we can easily see that digitalization amplifies the impact of information in social context when the goal is winning in a competition for resources.

Hence, we can put forward a second proposition:

Digitalization is a system for magnification of the impact of information by means of manipulation of information processing and information channels.

One of the benefits of unbiased digitalization is that it creates, *ceteris paribus*, a leveled playing field for its context – once a cost of access has been paid, the access is granted and there is no long-term competitive advantage that could be obtained by any of the groups. The situation reverses itself when two parties do not have an equal access to the resources provided by digitalization – in such scenario the most affluent group wins. Let us consider group A and group B, and let us assume that they have diametrically different political views. Under circumstances of group A having access only to text messaging, while group B having an access to text messaging, e-mail, phone calls, radio and TV, group B will prevail in the fight of messages with its opponent. Same goes for the situation where vendor of digitalization (e.g., a social network) is based against one of the groups comprising its context.

READER NOTES

Main points of agreement	
Supporting arguments (why agree?)	
Main points of disagreement	
Supporting arguments (why disagree?)	
Illustrative scenarios	
Possible research problem	
Possible research questions	

17

Digitalization and the Pressures of the Environment

The question regarding the forces acting between the environment and digitalization is fairly easy to answer – environment applies restrictive pressures to limit an expansive growth of digitalization, and digitalization exerts expansive, outward growth-oriented forces on its environment. Considering the fact that the digitalization and its environment are comprised of two fundamental sub-system – social and technical, we can identify two competing forces acting in opposite directions, in such way, that:

Internally, in *digitalization*:

- The *technical sub-system drives the expansion* of digitalization by optimization of the performance of the essential components, as well as by optimizing effectiveness and efficiency of the communication links between them. A modern assembly line, increasingly reliant on automation, is a good example of such expansion.
- The *social sub-system restricts the expansion* of digitalization driven by technical sub-system. This is only to be expected, for the purpose of a technical sub-system is to, eventually, replace and substitute its social counterpart. Consequently, given the demand for digitalization from its environment, the internal resistance would come from remaining people working in that system.

Externally, in the *environment*:

- The *social sub-system drives the expansion* of digitalization by providing an inviting target for more information channels. The continuous increase in the number of information channels is due to the

DOI: 10.1201/9781003304906-17

ever-thicker layering of the channels, where rarely a digital channel gets simply substituted by another channel. Instead, the social
sub-system keeps accumulating layers in its continuous effort to stay
current.

- The *technological sub-system restricts the expansion* of digitalization driven by "pull" demand of social sub-system of the environment. Given the benefits that digitalization provides to its context,
  the demand fuels expansion of digitalization. However, in order to
  accommodate the increasing immersion of social component into a
  digital domain, the appropriate technical infrastructure must be in
  place. And it is the absence of the well-developed and pervasive technical infrastructure, caused by such temporary limitations as the
  cost of technology and possible spatial-temporal restrictions, that
  slows the expansion of digitalization into its environment.

Let us start by stating an important proposition that we could use to
answer the question of "digitalization-context" interaction, as follows:

> A complex dynamic non-linear system has a tendency to change – to
> expand, spatially, within its environment, and to increase, internally, in its
> structural complexity.

Based on this proposition, we can posit the following implication:

> Social component of the context of digitalization will have a "pull" effect/
> response on digitalization that is conducive to the expansion of digitaliza-
> tion in its size and complexity.

We can perceive technical sub-system of the context as the interface
between the social sub-system and digitalization. Consequently, when
a demand from a social component increases, the new, or an improved,
interface is established, and digitalization "moves in" and the technical
sub-system expands by establishing a new A2D interface.

Simply put, digitalization will smoothly expand and integrate within an
appropriate technological part of its context, thus increasing its scope. The
examples are abundant – one may consider Apple's ecosystem of products,
which is based on the expansion of the number of products and services
provided by the same digital platform. We know that one of the barriers
to an increasing the immersion of users into its technological universe is

availability of the affordable infrastructure – specifically, hardware and software.

Given a finite pool of potential customers of digitalization, technological part of the context would have to rely, and exceedingly so, on increasing standardization of the technical interface – just like the existence and usage of the Internet is reliant on a set of standardized protocols. However, the standardization opens a door to competing systems of digitalization that could be considered attractive alternatives to the current and potential customers. This, in turn, may result in customer churn and the increased competition for consumers. It is only expected, then, that the reaction of the context would be preventive in nature – where the tools of digitalization would be concentrated under control of a few entities. And, obviously, this will contribute to further centralization of the core of the provision of the services of digitalization. All the while the appearance, the manifestation, of digitalization to a customer would be of highly decentralized and local nature.

This "centralized, really" but "decentralized, apparently" approach may result in return to host-based type of an architecture, where the processing is done at the center, and the customers are given the illusion of decentralization via kiosks and dumb terminals. This, incidentally, will lower the barriers to entry into the world of digitalization for all and any potential customers. Despite the conversations regarding the demise of the Google-type data centers and incoming dominance of Edge computing, it is hard to imagine such implementation being practical for a large number of customers.

The response of the social component of the environment of digitalization is more nuanced and complex. Let us consider, in the next chapter, some of the obvious scenarios and possible responses to the scenarios that may develop under two basic environmental assumptions.

READER NOTES

Main points of agreement	
Supporting arguments (why agree?)	
Main points of disagreement	
Supporting arguments (why disagree?)	
Illustrative scenarios	
Possible research problem	
Possible research questions	

18

Digitalization and Non-Competitive Context

Let us begin this chapter by considering an example that is based on the following assumption:

> Social environment is homogeneous – the residents are mutually non-competitive.

An obvious example for such scenario is a *digital consumer*, who is not even aware of the presence of other consumers in the digital market-place – an interaction with digitalization with the purpose of purchasing a product does not require such awareness. Another simple example of such environment is digitalization services provided to music listeners, or mobile gamers, where lovers of country music coexist peacefully with listeners of classic music, and the players who like Game A do not feel any animosity towards their counterparts that prefer Game B.

In such cases, homogeneity of the social component of the environment of digitalization *does not mean that all participants of the social component are alike.* Instead, this assumption implies the *absence of competition* between the participants and the sub-groups of the social component that are capable of impacting "digitalization-to-context" interaction. However, as we will see, the possible responses to some of the scenarios will contribute to the stratification of the social component of the context of digitalization.

Scenario 1: *Continuous increase* in the delivery of relative value received from the impact of digitalization. For example, a smartphone offers a lot of value with a little management overhead. This leads to the growth in the number and quality of digital information channels

DOI: 10.1201/9781003304906-18

available to the social component. A possible response to this scenario is a resultant growth of digitalization via creation of new A2D interfaces by technical component prompted by "pull" effect resulting from the demand from social component.

Scenario 2: *Gradual decrease* in the delivery of relative value of digitalization brought about by the increasing complexity of technical component of the environment and digitalization. Under such scenario, digitalization still provides a lot of value to consumers, but the process is corresponded by a continuously increasing management overhead. This could be because any further increase in an on-line presence requires the customer to manage and to attend to profiles on multiple sites and platforms. But, eventually, the law of diminishing returns kicks in and the growth in the number of digital information channels reaches a saturation point.

A possible response to the second scenario results in *reduction in growth* of digitalization due to increasing complexity of management of the technical component by social component. However, a more likely response manifests in the form of *continuous growth* of digitalization by means of introducing an additional layer of technology responsible for managing the increase in complexity. This is an attempt of hiding the actual complexity of digitalization from the customers behind the apparently simple interface. This type of a response is exemplified by a wide-spread adaptation of voice command-based smart speakers (e.g., Alexa, Echo, etc.) by the customers.

Scenario 3: *Significant decrease* in the delivery of *relative* value of digitalization brought about by the substitution of the analog channels characterizing face-to-face social interactions by the digitally mediated social interactions. This scenario signifies an attempt of the customers to return to their "native" analog state, and to prioritize local analog interactions *vis-à-vis* global digital ones. Such scenario would be met by the actions coming not only from social component, but from technical component as well. Let us take a look at the possible responses to this scenario.

Social component's response to a significant decrease in relative value delivered by digitalization may rely on an attempt to re-capture some of the analog channels used in social interactions as a reaction to the perceived decrease in quality of life. Conscious attempt to minimize the number of digital channels by the customers may lead to customers becoming "digital renegades" – this could manifest in customers abandoning their digital social network accounts and joining an analog interest-based local social group.

Digitalization's response to such scenario is via consolidation of the multiple digital channels into a smaller (e.g., aiming for a necessary minimum of one) number of channels via reduction in the number of information pathways and reduction in the number of analog channels that require A2D conversion. A possible example of such response is an introduction of a single sign-on system in a corporate system, or a single Microsoft sign-on to access a variety of applications. This response is also an effort to create an appearance of apparent simplicity of digitalization to its customers, while hiding the actual complexity of the system. The approach is similar to that of "as long as this car runs no one needs to be concerned how it runs and what, exactly, is under the hood".

However, it is also possible that a significant decrease in relative value delivered by digitalization to its customers would result in a different reaction. Consumers may undertake continuous attempts to substitute lost analog channels of face-to-face interactions by continuously improving, wider and faster, digital channels. Such approach can be referred to as "chasing the digital high" and it would result in an inevitable increase in the number of digital information channels used by a customer. An interesting question, of course, is how many digital information channels represent a breaking point – how many is "too many channels"? The answer is, of course, context-dependent, where two different people may have a different number of channels after which the changes in behavior are due. Thus, it is possible that an answer lies in some form of ratio or could be represented as an index of some sort.

The problem, however, is that there is an obvious limit to the number of digital channels that the consumers may utilize – even the best multitaskers are bound to hit the wall. Thus, a reasonable response of technical component is by means of continuous consolidation of the multiple A2D channels into, eventually, a single one. This could be done in order to simplify the mode of access of digitalization by social component of the environment and vice versa. This is an example where everything would become controllable via, let us say, a single app on a smartphone. Another route is via proliferation of such transparent A2D interfaces as bio sensors – this would also create a perception of simplicity and will hide the actual complexity of digitalization behind the curtain.

For the system of digitalization, however, the general trend for growth and development seems to be fairly straightforward – it is the path of relying on expansion and substitution. Namely, a continuous expansion of digitalization into technical component of its context leads the way in promoting and creating ubiquity of offerings based on the model of A2D conversion. This will be corresponded by strong attempts leading towards a continuous substitution of the analog-based decentralized decision making of the social component by the centralized decision making of digitalization.

Based on the outlined progression of the scenarios, we are justified to suggest the following outcomes:

In the case of the homogeneous socio-technical context, the impact of digitalization results in stratification of the social component into three layers:

1. *"Digital renegades", which are those who eventually reject those aspects of the digitalization that are under their control and make attempts to reduce the number of digital channels*
2. *"Digital converts", which are those who embrace all the aspects of digitalization and who continuously upgrade their digital infrastructure and continuously reduce the number of analog channels in their lives*
3. *"Digital moderates", which are those who follow a "middle path" to digitalization and view it as a tool that has its pluses and minuses*

We must make an important note regarding the aspects of digitalization that are "under control" of the social component – the pressure of digitalization on its environment must proceed along the lines of maximizing the number of indispensable channels and minimizing the number of discretionary channels. For example, let us consider a *digital renegade* who can only make his medical appointments and refill his prescription via using the Internet, or who must conduct her affair relying on an on-line banking in order to pay her bills and to receive her pay.

It is likely, in both of the cases, that despite the intent of some of the customer directed at "going back to analog", the corresponding digital channels will remain well-utilized, for those channels are not really discretionary, but, rather, they became essential to the well-being and functioning of individuals within a society. Meaning, the price to pay for not having some of the channels is prohibitively expensive. On the other hand, a person who has a subscription to a newspaper (a hard copy version or a digital one) may very well opt out of receiving "breaking news" updates on her phone, thus eliminating a discretionary information channel from an already large collection of the available ones.

READER NOTES

Main points of agreement	
Supporting arguments (why agree?)	
Main points of disagreement	
Supporting arguments (why disagree?)	
Illustrative scenarios	
Possible research problem	
Possible research questions	

19

Digitalization and Competitive Context

Let us now consider a different scenario that brings some additional complexity to digitalization and its context, where:

Social Environment is heterogeneous – the residents are mutually competitive.

In the case of this scenario, heterogeneity of the context does not mean that the individuals comprising the context are different. Instead, heterogeneity implies *the presence of the multiple groups that are characterized by competing interests*. This case of the environment is especially important and interesting for three reasons. First, this condition of the environment is more likely to be encountered in a real world of *digital activists*, second, because it is under this condition the behavior of digitalization could become chaotic. Third, and the most importantly, this scenario may lead to *weaponization of digitalization*.

Let us consider some obvious scenarios and possible responses to the scenarios, which take place in the case if:

1. The main goal is the *creation* of a new group.
2. The main goal is the *survival* of the group that is *dependent* on other groups.
3. The main goal of the group is the *domination* of the opponents.
4. The main goal of the group is the *elimination* of the opponents.

In this chapter we take a look at the first two scenarios, and the other two will be covered in the next chapter.

Scenario 1: Creation of a new, stand alone, group.

DOI: 10.1201/9781003304906-19

It is important to note that *the social context is not an unlimited resource* because there is a finite number of possible participants. As a result, the consequence of creating a new group results in a competition for the resources that humans possess – time, money, energy, and so on. Consequently, even if a new group is to be created without any intention to compete for resources with any other group (e.g., book club, macramé society, etc.), it will end up doing so, because the existence of a new group is based on a participation of its members, where the members must dedicate their resources to sustaining the group. This does not have to be anything drastic, because the resources have to be allocated even toward such, often taken for granted, means as responding to e-mails, participating in on-line forums, and so on.

A possible social response to the first scenario is via creating a new analog identity for the group, technological response is by creating a new A2D interface, and the response of digitalization is by means of creating new information channels and the digital version of the group's identity. This scenario represents the best possible option for an expansion of digitalization, because all the competition for the resources takes place in an analog domain, so, the digital domain simply scales up by creating more corresponding digital identities.

> *Scenario 2: Creation of a new group intended to co-exist with (e.g., integrate with, or reference) other existing groups and to share the available resources with those groups.*

An example for such scenario is the creation of a fan group for a star athlete, which is dependent on, first, referencing his team and, second, the league where his team plays. This is inevitable, because a new identity, a new group, could only be established in reference to some other identity or a group. Additionally, there must be a link to groups that are alike as well as to the groups that are different. This is done in order to support the identity of the new group by saying "We are different from this group, but we have a common ground with that group".

Under this scenario, the existence of a new group is based on, and is partially dependent on, the presence of other groups. Consequently, a new group must identify a sub-set of resources that could be poached from existing groups.

Given the second scenario, a social response could proceed by creating a:

- Unique identity for the subject of the interest to the group, and

- Shared identity characterized by the linkage of the new identity to the established identity, or to an identity of other group(s).

Let us imagine, for example, that we are interested in creating a fan group for Baseball Star, who is a current player in MLB, who likes his dog Sparky, and who is also very fashionable – a good dresser. A combination of the three aspects of Baseball Star – baseball, dog, and fashion – provide a somewhat unique social identity of the person. But, in order to grow the membership of the group beyond a few dedicated fans, a set of shared identities must also be created. The baseball aspect must be linked to the particular team Baseball Star plays to, or to MLB in general. Then, the "dog-loving" aspect would be linked to a fan group of the particular breed of the dog, and the "fashion side" of Baseball Star may be linked to the luxury/fashion houses selling the clothing, or some fan groups of particular items (e.g., if Baseball Star likes rare sneakers, then it could be an association with a club dedicated to sneakerheads).

What about technical response? Technical response is via provision of the digital interface needed for A2D translation. Specifically, the response of digitalization is by:

- Placing the synergistic groups on the same digital platform, and
- Creating an interlinked digital eco-system.

If we continue with our example of fashionable and dog-loving MLB player, then the new fan group residing in the digital domain would have to assure, in order to grow, that whatever digital content it houses could be presented to all interested parties in a consistent way and does not require any additional efforts for the visitors to expend. Additionally, the domain hosting the site itself would need to provide reliable links to other domains linking Baseball Star to the synergistic groups without requiring any additional efforts to access them. Meaning, if a visitor follows a link, then it should not require the interested person to register, or to pay a fee, or encounter a warning that the site is for "Members Only".

The first two scenarios discussed above are the preferred ones for digitalization. The reason is simple – in both cases the objective is growth of the social group in both, analog and digital domain, and, most importantly, the objective is a *balanced* growth. This means that as analog presence of a social group expands in a larger social context, its digital presence in the domain of digitalization expands as well – the process of expansion is reminiscent of self-reinforcing feedback loop. In both cases, a social component opens wide the doors to digitalization via provision of the demand for digital representation. And, this "pull" effect allows digitalization to pour in and expand into newly created and available space.

In the case of the last two scenarios, however, the balanced growth is not possible – let us take a closer look at the underlying reasons in the next chapter.

READER NOTES

Main points of agreement	
Supporting arguments (why agree?)	
Main points of disagreement	
Supporting arguments (why disagree?)	
Illustrative scenarios	
Possible research problem	
Possible research questions	

20

Digitalization and Adversarial Social Groups

Let us now consider a set of different scenarios that may take place in the case when the balanced growth of digitalization is not possible. Namely, in the situations where the main goal of the new group is a:

- *Domination of the opponents* and/or
- *Elimination of the opponents.*

Unfortunately, the two scenarios are exceedingly likely if we accept the fact that in a lot of cases, human beings are driven by other principles and interests then rationality and utility. And once we do accept this premise, it opens a door to a very large selection of reasons for why humans may behave passionately and not necessarily reasonably.

Let us consider the first scenario of this chapter, as follows:

Scenario 3: Creation of a new group intended to dominate other groups of its kind and to dominate the associated pool of the available resources.

A possible example for such scenario is a creation of a group supporting a challenger to the incumbent *within the same political party*. Under this scenario, a new group must end up with the new analog and digital identities for their subject of interest, namely, the person who the group supports. But, this is done under the condition where the created identities of the challenger are neither independent, nor complementary, but rather *adversarial* to those of the competitor. However, because the concept of domination requires having the same base for all the groups involved in such competition, the path of a total destruction of the opponents is not available.

DOI: 10.1201/9781003304906-20

Consider, as an example, two statements:

- Football team A dominates its opponents within their league.
- Football team A dominated baseball team B, while team B dominated soccer team C.

While the second statement makes a little, if any sense to any sports fan, it is possible to accept the first statement. This is because football team A, and all of the opponents, have a common base – the game of football played within the same league – NFL. If, indeed, football team A is so good as to practically destroy its competitors as to leave them no chance for winning, then *there will be no game any longer*, and there would be no competition for anyone to watch and participate in. In a similar fashion, when two politicians from the same party go head on, they cannot adopt a "scorched earth" approach, for they do have a common ground that they both must stand on.

The social response in the case of this scenario is two-fold, because it requires creating two identities for the subject of interest:

- First, the group must create a new and unique identity clearly differentiating the subject (e.g., *we are special and we are good!*).
- Second, the group must create a shared identity characterized by the linkage of the new identity to the established one of the other group of groups (e.g., *we are especially special and good in comparison and relatively to the other group*).

There is also a response from a technical component, where the response is via a provision of the interface to digitalization. Similarly, the response of digitalization is two-fold, via:

- Placing the competing groups on the same digital platform, and
- Creating an interlinked digital eco-system.

This is similar to placing two tennis players on the same court, and enforcing the rules of the game for both. Digitally, the analogy is to prevent one of the teams playing a video game against another team from using a newly discovered hack to score points. All the players, all the teams must play the same game and abide by the same rules.

The problem, however, is that such approach threatens the orderly functioning of the system of digitalization, which requires the presence of some sort of diversity for growth, and where any attrition of the "digital residents" will contribute to shrinking of digitalization and of scope of its context. Let us consider, as an example, Twitter as a digital platform, that hosts Republican and Democratic users. There are three options.

- First, it is possible to have Republican Twitter and Democratic Twitter, but not for long, because the eventual homogeneity of either group will bring the end to the participation of the analog residents – a homogeneous environment holds no surprises and presents a limited interest. Information value is limited, eventually.
- Second, Twitter may allow for the presence of the both group and practice non-interference. This path will lead to the escalation of the adversarial activities, with the eventual outcome of the reduced participation of the analog residents. As an analogy let us consider a new road, that, over time, becomes very popular, but more and more dangerous and unpleasant to drive by the commuters – such road, eventually, will become less and less utilized. There has to be a balance, of some sort.
- Finally, there is an option of controlling the digital domain with the purpose of managing the adversarial and competing digital identities – this is, pretty much, the path of action we are getting to witness now.

The three options above lead to the following consequences:

- Digital isolationism and strict compartmentalization of the cyberspace
- Increasing complexity of interactions leading to chaotic behavior of digitalization
- Tight autocratic control by means of censorship, management, and rights-based privileges

This scenario is still based on the presence of multiple co-existing groups, regardless of their competition for the available resources. Consequently, even if a given group obtains a dominating position in this competition, it still requires the presence of other group(s).

Let us consider Player A who competes against Player B, and let us consider that Player A is winning the competition. If Player A is so strong as to completely dominate Player B, then the game is not interesting to observe or to participate in for either of two players. If, however, the players are more evenly matched so the winning of one player is not guaranteed, then the game is worth participating and watching. Thus, even if one social group aims to dominate another group or groups, it will still have to, for practical reasons, leave those other groups enough resources to assure their viability. After all, in this scenario one group wants to obtain a dominating position *vis-à-vis* the other group or groups. The next general scenario, however, is not based on the principles of "winning a fair fight", but on an extreme pragmatic or ideological premises, and, as a result, it is the most problematic scenario to deal with.

> *Scenario 4: Creation of a new group intended to eliminate other groups and to assert a complete control over the pool of the available resources.*

A good example for this scenario is the creation of any group that operates under the assumption of *zero-sum game* – where the goal is to exterminate the opponent and to come up on top, or, otherwise, to be destroyed. Modern day's Presidential elections follow, pretty much, a similar route.

But, if we look closer, then this scenario has sub-scenarios – specifically, there are two options:

- *Scenario 4.1 – where the winning party is satisfied with the win without needing to make their victory known to the public,* and
- *Scenario 4.2 – where the winning party wants to make their victory known to the public.*

Let us take those scenarios and look at them in order.

First, regarding *Scenario 4.1,* there is an option of creating an isolated group, in both analog and digital domains. Meaning, a terrorist or a conspiracy organization bent on destroying its opponents is likely to conduct its affairs in a closed to outsiders analog (read, social) domain, where no outsider can simply walk in and join the group or take a part in a conversation between the members of the group. Similarly, such group could establish its own restricted digital domain, which will be isolated from the rest of the publicly available content on the Internet by various protective means. Based on this scenario, even if such pragmatics- or ideology-driven group wants to completely dominate the playing field and aims to destroy its opponents, *it is not emphasizing the public aspect of their fight* – such organization could be perfectly happy with achieving a resounding victory without having an audience to witness it. Let us say, a home owner fights vermin that invaded his house. Exterminators came in, solved the problem, and all is well. But, the home owner is not bent on the idea of disseminating the message around the neighborhood that he prevailed in that battle.

If we continue the same line of thought, then it is fair to say that Sinaloa cartel does not want to be simply stronger, or does not even want to dominate its rival Juarez cartel. Instead, Sinaloa cartel wants to destroy its competitor and to take over Juarez's business without any need for a public forum-like open discussion regarding the relative virtues of the involved parties. Some terrorist organizations want to blow up an airliner full of people and they want the whole world to know about it and who did it. Yet another terrorist organization may want to deploy a dirty bomb in the middle of a city and would prefer for the perpetrator to remain anonymous to the public. All that matters are results. It is a well-known fact, by now, that criminal and terrorist organizations use, and successfully so, digital domain to conduct their affair. From the perspective of digitalization such scenario is not surprising at all, and, indeed, it is very similar to the first scenario outlined above – digitalization simply offers an extension of analog domain providing all the benefits of digital data communication and processing. The important point of note: the resultant digital domain is *limited by design*.

Similar to *Scenario 3*, social response proceeds in phases. First phase is dedicated to creating a digital counterpart of the analog identity of the group, and the second phase is geared towards creating a protected from the outsiders' digital domain for the digital identity of the group – this could be easily handled by security and privacy-oriented policies and procedures of the group. The last phase is dedicated to establishing a link connecting the group and the general public, which is necessary for conquering and claiming the resources of the defeated or destroyed counterpart. Technical response is via provision of the interface to digitalization, establishing protective mechanisms around the digital domain of the group, and the corresponding channels of communications. The response of digitalization is via creating an isolated digital eco-system for the group.

The last scenario we are going to consider, *Scenario 4.2,* is much more problematic and consequential, because it is associated with creating or expanding an ideological group that aims at destroying its perceived opponents *while being intentionally visible* within a public domain. Sometimes, the intended audience is artificially expanded to include as many digital residents as possible – this is an example of *digitalization functioning in broadcast mode.* As an example, we could consider a group that is Pro-Life (or, conversely, Pro-Choice) in its political and social persuasions, aiming to, first, dominate, and then, to destroy its opponent in public space – both analog and digital. Same could be said about the groups representing radical Left and radical Right political parties, where the simple defeat of an opposition is not enough, for what is required is a complete annihilation of the opponent performed in the public space for everyone to observe.

This scenario, for all intents and purposes, is not entirely unlike and is, in fact, a rehashing of the practices of inquisition, where the trial is conducted in secrecy, but the execution of the designated ideological heretics must take place in the largest public place available to the executioner. Such situation becomes problematic for digitalization, because what is required of it is creating and maintaining a public digital space populated with mutually adversarial and outright hostile digital identities. This requires a single system to exist not only in sub-optimal configuration, but to exist in the state of multiple competing configurations – and this, as we shall see later, may lead to a chaotic behavior of the whole system.

This brings up a very important issue – that of stability of digitalization, where a group could derive a short term competitive advantage over other groups via a continuous flow of new messages practically clogging the available information channels. Thus, instead of providing an increased longevity of the information and of the messages, digitalization, actually, *shortens a life span of the messages.* This also contributes to continuously decreasing stability of digitalization. Thus, we put forward another proposition:

> In the case of the presence of multiple social groups competing for available shared pool of resources digitalization will become unstable.

An analogy for such scenario is a distributed denial of service attack, where a Web server simply becomes overwhelmed with the amount of incoming messages, or a condition of "thrashing" of the system implementing virtual memory that is caused by more requests for "swapping" than the OS and the processor can handle.

Social response to this sub-scenario is three-fold, because it requires creating three identities for the subject of interest.

1. First, the group must create a new and unique identity clearly differentiating the subject. This is an *intragroup* representation of the subject that is created for the purposes of "internal consumption" of the homogeneous group that the subject belongs to. For example, Mark, a new challenger from Democratic party, would have his first identity created to show his fellow Democrats why he is a better choice to run.

   - Second, the group must create a shared identity characterized by the linkage of the new identity to the established one of the other group. This is an *intergroup* identity that is created for the purpose of demonstrating why the subject is a well-suited to fight against the representatives of the competing group. Continuing our example with Mark, the second identity would be created to portray Mark not as a better Democrat, but a better Democrat who could beat his Republican opponents.

   - Finally, the third identity would be created for the purposes of the representation of the subject in a wide open marketplace. The goal of the third identity is to hide the specifics, as well as possible associated rough edges, of the first and second identities, so the subject appears in the most general positive light to the largest context possible. The most palatable representation to the general public, in a sense. In the case of our example of Mark, the third identity would be the one that is appealing to those citizens who are registered Independent. And, this is a difficult identity to create...

Technical response is via provision of the interface to digitalization. The response of digitalization is via placing the competing groups on their respective digital platforms, and creating a carefully interlinked digital eco-system. In the case of Mark, technical response would include:

- Mark's digital platform is geared toward Democrats.
- Mark's digital platform is geared toward his fight against Republicans.
- Mark's digital platform is geared toward Independent voters.
- Mark's digital eco-system allows a limited interconnection between the three platforms.

The problem, of course, is related to the filtering of the information flows – where supporters of Mark would want to keep certain information about their candidate strictly within one of the platforms. It is doubtful that such control could be accomplished strictly by technological means – it is not possible to limit the semantic content purely on the basis of syntactic filters.

Consequently, a social interference and supervision would be required to implement such instance of digitalization.

This is bound to result in continuing increase in complexity of digitalization and its behavior. Let us consider an example of a project where three teams work on a design of a car. Further, three teams have competing and conflicting ideas of what a good design should be. The first group considers a good car to be a fast car that can be raced on a track. The second group is of an opinion that a good car should allow its passengers to travel in comfort and luxury. The third group is all about fuel efficiency and "green" energy. The best option for such teams is to create three different designs, for their respective perspectives differ significantly. However, the teams are made to work together on a single design. As practice demonstrates, such projects often become chaotic, for we don't do well in dealing with multi-criteria objectives.

So, in the next chapter we take a look at some of the implications of increasing complexity of structure and behavior on digitalization.

READER NOTES

Main points of agreement	
Supporting arguments (why agree?)	
Main points of disagreement	
Supporting arguments (why disagree?)	
Illustrative scenarios	
Possible research problem	
Possible research questions	

21

Managing a Conflict Environment of Digitalization

The purpose of this chapter is to discuss the nature and sources of a conflict associated with (and brought about by) the increasing structural complexity of digitalization during the process of significant transformative change. For our purposes, we define transformative change as *any purposeful change associated with the goal-driven alteration of the behavior and the structure of the system*. In the case of digitalization, this could be caused by the expansion of the system into a new context – in the case of consumers this could be moving towards serving new customers, with new set of socio-cultural expectations, technological capabilities, communicating in a new language. Or, this could be due to scaling up a social network during the period of significant social, cultural, and political changes (e.g., elections). There are multiple reasons for conflicts, some of them are generic, and some are specific to a given setting. We suggest the existence of two types of risk factors associated with the conflicts that are relevant to digitalization.

The first type refers to contextual risk factors, which are specific to a given setting and are unique to each instance of using digitalization. As a result, they are difficult to identify in advance. The second type refers to inherent risk factors that are common to all complex socio-technical systems. These inherent risk factors could be and should be foreseen and anticipated during the period of any significant change. We suggest that one of the inherent risk factors is associated with the complexity of the structure of digitalization, and we intend to demonstrate that under specific circumstances the increasing structural complexity of a system can give rise to a chaotic behavior of the system. Which, in turn, is associated with the loss of control and creation of the conflict-prone environment.

DOI: 10.1201/9781003304906-21

Let us consider a general example – an example of a complex system that aims to withstand a new set of pressures from its environment. In order to survive, the system must acquire a new set of functionalities – to change its original behavior. Changes in the behavior are usually enabled, or supported, by the changes in the internal architecture of the system – its structure. If the environmental pressures are diverse enough to require very different, or even conflicting, behavioral responses, then such system could become chaotic during the process of its reorganization.

It is important to note that the process of a transformative change is a part of a wave-like pattern, where the beginning of the process is characterized by the "unfreezing" of the structure of the system at the beginning, then "moving" to a new, more complex structure required to support new functionalities, and then "refreezing" the new structure via efforts to reduce the increased complexity to the minimum. This process repeats itself when a period of a new transformative change comes along.

In this chapter, we rely on two important assumptions that:

1. *An order and the absence of a conflict are associated with the presence of control over the behavior of a socio-technical system (e.g., digitalization)*
2. *A chaos and the presence of a conflict are associated with the absence of control over the behavior of the system.*

The link between the complexity of the structure and complexity of the behavior justifies the fundamental assumption that *more complex socio-technical structures are more conflict-prone then the less complex ones.*

In our consideration we do not deal with the issues of a conflict resolution directly; rather, we inquire into the issue of *the management of the environment for the purposes of conflict resolution.*

Our unit of analysis is an "actor-digitalization" interaction, and the focus is a complexity of the behavior of digitalization that is caused by the changes in demands of the actors who instantiated the interaction.

Let us consider a social network during an election year to be our example of digitalization. This system is instantiated by the interaction of the system with digital activists, which have conflicting and sometime adversarial, interests. In order to thrive, the social network must accommodate different groups on the same platform, which will result in a necessary overlap of the information channels of those groups. Which, in turn, will result in the increasing complexity of the interactions – this could be, of course, easily remedied via compartmentalization of each group. However, this is not a preferred option for those actors who desire to publicly dominate their opponents and to demonstrate that their own beliefs and values triumph over those held by their opponents.

We state the general question we are interested in exploring as follows:

> What are some of the means that may allow for management of the complexity of the behavior of digitalization?

In our quest for an answer we adapt a two-phase approach. First, we argue that *Chaos Theory* can provide a solid theoretical foundation for looking at the behavior of digitalization. We premise this argument on the basis that digitalization can be perceived as a complex non-linear dynamic system with a pattern of behavior that falls under the purview of Chaos Theory. Second, we argue that *Complex System Theory* can provide important insights regarding the management of the complexity of the behavior of digitalization. The foundation of the argument is the premise that *complex systems exhibit self-organizing behavior that can be indirectly manipulated through the management of interdependencies between the system's components.*

The justification of the selected approach is intuitive, for a theoretical foundation can offer a generalized perspective on a context-dependent subject. Meaning, this would allow us for having a common ground in investigating and comparing instances of digitalization in the USA, Europe, Asia, or Africa. The reason for using two theoretical perspectives on complex systems is quite simple also: while Chaos Theory offers insights regarding the behavior of complex systems, it does not deal with the *management* of that behavior. Consequently, we use Complex Systems Theory to get insights regarding the ways by which the behavior of a complex system can be managed. Given the selected theoretical foundation, we can unfold the general question into two specific questions, as follows:

- *What insights can Chaos Theory offer regarding the behavior of digitalization?*
- *What insights can Complex System Theory provide regarding the management of that behavior?*

We begin with an overview of the characteristics of non-linear dynamic systems and of the major tenets of Chaos Theory. Let us recall that the major premise of our perspective is that:

digitalization is a complex non-linear dynamic system behavior of which can become chaotic, but can also be managed by manipulation of interdependencies between the system's components.

We can summarize the basic characteristics of complex non-linear dynamic systems as follows:

- A system is *complex* if it consists of a large number of interacting components.
- The interactions between the components of a complex system are associated with the presence of a feedback mechanism, which, due to the non-linearity of the feedback-controlled interactions, makes a complex system itself *non-linear* and causes it to exhibit/develop *emergent properties* (e.g., appearance of independently observable and empirically verifiable patterns of the collective behavior of the system).
- Complex system is *dynamic* if its state or behavior changes with time.
- Complex system is *deterministic* in terms of the cause and effect, if the variables describing it relate to each other in a non-probabilistic way.

Chaos Theory can be defined as a *qualitative study of unstable aperiodic behavior in deterministic non-linear dynamical systems*. Consequently, a subject of study of Chaos Theory is a large class of complex systems capable of exhibiting chaotic pattern of behavior. Behavior of a system can be represented in terms of an *attractor*, or a set of points in the phase space of a dynamical feedback system that defines its steady state motion. Every attractor has a *basin of attraction*, or a set of points in the space of system variables that evolve to a particular attractor. Aperiodically fluctuating systems are said to have a *strange attractor*. Strange attractors are *chaotic* when the trajectories in the phase space, from two points very close on the attractor, diverge exponentially due to the system's sensitive dependence on initial conditions and small perturbations in control parameters.

We may consider an example of an application of the concept of an attractor to digitalization. In the case of actors instantiating the system of digitalization, a system's attractor could be represented by a particular pattern of interaction with the system. This pattern would have certain characteristics, such as when the most purchase orders are placed, when the most inquiries regarding the deliveries are submitted, and so on. And this pattern would change based on the changes in the context. After all, we don't expect shopping patterns that take place during a week to be distributed evenly, and we do not expect that Christmas/holiday shopping period will have the same pattern as an off season does. In a similar fashion, in the case of a social network we expect a difference in the patterns of communication of its members based on the changes in socio-political climate, or in the case of the expansion of the reach of the social network into the new social contexts.

According to Chaos Theory, complex systems may:

1. have multiple attractors associated with multiple patterns of behavior, and
2. transition from a semi-stable to a chaotic state.

The entry into a chaotic state takes place when a value of a *key parameter of a system* increases and exceeds a threshold value, forcing a single outcome basin to expand into two distinct causal fields. This process of *bifurcation* can safely continue up to the point of a system having eight basins of attraction. However, the next bifurcation marks the onset of *chaos*.

Note: It is an interesting research question to investigate – what is the key parameter for a given system of digitalization within its context? What would push a particular system into behaving chaotically?

From the perspective of Chaos Theory, a transformation of a socio-technical system can be viewed as the process of matching the actual state of a system with the intended one by means of manipulating the behavior of the existing system. In terms of Chaos Theory, the process of transformation is concerned with a transformation of the current system's state to a new dynamical state. We know that when a system goes through the process of consecutive bifurcations, the number of its natural outcomes, or states, changes. However, internal structural parameters of the system stay the same. Consequently, in a *pre-chaotic* region the same internal configuration of the system might produce up to eight different outcomes. However, as the system enters a state of chaos, new windows of order appear; this represents the emergence of entirely new forms of a socio-technical system.

Note: Does this mean that a social network that hosts more than eight social groups with conflicting interests may end up behaving chaotically? If not, then what is the limit in terms of having the number of conflicting groups? Or, the only way is to let digitalization to become an open ground dominated by warring clans?

The implications are obvious – if we desire an entirely different socio-technical arrangement of digitalization, then the process of the transformation *must* go through the chaotic stage, which makes the system's environment more susceptible to conflicts. Meaning, if a social digital platform is intended to expand from having, let us say, two groups with dissimilar perspective on the same subject, then opening its platform to eight or more may result in encountering and navigating through some troubled waters.

For the purposes of this discussion, we can define a *conflict* within a context of digitalization as an *emergent, detrimental social and/or socio-technical interaction that is associated with and triggered by the process of the goal-oriented structural transformation*. This is not to say that this reason for a conflict is *the only reason* – instead, there are could be a multitude of reasons (e.g., personal, hardware-based (e.g., natural disaster strikes), software-based (e.g., DDOS), policy/procedures-based (e.g., sudden change in policy), and so on) for a conflict. But, for the purposes of our discussion we concentrate on this specific one. Let us consider an example of conflict by using our previous hypothetical scenario of a social network in an election year.

Suppose, we have three groups of activists aligned with three politicians that advocate very different socio-economic messages. Only one of the politicians can be elected for an office. It is not difficult to imagine that if given the "information commons", then the digital information channels of the activists would intersect, thus creating a common pool of (possibly, negative, and perhaps, contradictory) information. Such information environment cannot be characterized as friendly, instead, the messages will become more and more hostile, reflecting the increasingly adversarial attitudes of activists. To prevent the resultant discord and hostility, the social network uses moderators to block certain informational content generated by those activists that moderators deem hostile. Such manipulation of the information channels is an example of a structural transformation of the social network, which would result in the state of conflict with the censored activists and their readers/followers.

Our definition of a *conflict* leads us to two propositions:

Proposition 1:

The process of transformation aiming to obtain a qualitatively new form of digitalization will take place in a conflict-prone environment. Conversely, if the goal of the transformation is to change the behavior of digitalization while preserving the existing structure, then the process of transformation does not have to have a chaotic part, which makes the socio-technical environment less susceptible to conflicts.

Proposition 2:

The process of socio-technical transformation aiming to change the behavior of digitalization, while preserving the existing structure, does not have to take place in conflict-prone environment.

It is important to note, that even if the process described in Proposition 2 *could become chaotic*, according to Chaos Theory this process *does not have to become chaotic*, while the process described in Proposition 1 does.

Again, let us consider an illustrative example. In the case of a social network that is attempting to grow within its environment, the growth would require accommodating more and more participants on its platform. Such expansion, inevitably, invites multiple groups of active members with diverging interests and messages, and every group could be said to require its own structural socio-technical configuration managed by the administration/moderators. Again, let us keep in mind that any attempt to "subnet" the information space via compartmentalizing the social network would not work well, because active "netizens" are interested in promoting their ideas vis-à-vis participants from the other groups. So, given the expanding universe of the social network, in order to accommodate multiple co-located groups the system would have to be in the state characterized by multiple socio-technical configuration. Once the number of the configurations hits the threshold, the network *must* slip into behaving chaotically. In other words, an orderly discussion *must* deteriorate into being a digital shouting match filled with words in caps and emojis.

Next, let us attempt to identify the ways of managing the behavior of digitalization that is about to enter, has entered, or emerges from the chaotic state. Three requirements are essential for managing the behavior of a chaotic system:

1. Understanding of non-linearity,
2. Appreciation of the sensitivity of the system to its initial conditions, and
3. Understanding of a non-average behavior as a source of change.

Concerning the first requirement, it is of great importance to find the *leverages* or *lever points* of the system that could be subject to *butterfly effect*. Once these leverages are found, even a small targeted change may produce larger scale results compared to comprehensive change efforts that may squelch an organization's or social system's capacity for adaptive response. And while it is not a trivial task to find the system's leverage points, the best approach is to use multiple possible leverages and hope that at least some of them will work. Let us consider a simple example of non-linearity as it applies to a social network – the case of viral messages. Such messages produce a disproportionate impact, where a feedback mechanism causes them to be re-send again and again and again. In a similar fashion, a blocking of some of the posts and/or accounts by the administration or a moderator may cause a similarly disproportionate reaction from the members of the network.

Note: What could serve as lever points in the system of digitalization? What sort of actions made by the system have a disproportionate effect on its context? What could pacify the agitated group of the members of the social network whose subject matter has been banned? What can ease the anger of the customers who did not receive their order, or a response from the customer service?

The second requirement, a system's sensitivity to initial conditions, raises concerns regarding the effectiveness of the commonly utilized practices of benchmarking and the transfer of best practices. According to Chaos Theory, we cannot expect the same intervention to produce the same effect in two different systems, and the suggestion that managers identify the elements unique to their environments prior to the implementation of another jurisdiction's best practice seems to be well warranted. If applied to the case of digitalization, then it may mean that the system functioning well in one context, may not do so in a different context. Meaning, a successful on-line retailer selling work wear, should not expect a problem-free transition to selling fashion item if relying on the established system for selling work wear.

Note: What are the ways of identifying what, specifically, a given context represents vis-à-vis other ones? Would a social network, if launched in Germany, benefit from the experience of the best practices it identified in the USA? Would a retailer expanding to Asia transfer the experience to its digital branch in Africa?

The last requirement refers to the appreciation for a non-average, unusual event that pushes the boundaries of existing structures and processes and leads the way for new forms of organizational response and evolution after bifurcating events. Such an event will most likely manifest itself in the form of an outlier, produced by a complex system with the pattern of the behavior that is neither normally distributed nor regular. There are plenty of example for such events in the case of digitalization. In the case of consumers ordering a product, this could be a sudden delay in order processing and delivery during a holiday season, or it could be a sudden rush of orders for an obscure and not previously popular item, or a wave of returns/complaints/cancellations due to the previously unknown flaw in the product. In the case of the activists, such event could be exemplified by a discovery of a partiality or bias on the part of the social network, or by an external socio-political calamity caused by (or associated with – justly or not) or attributed to a sub-set of activists with the opposing views.

Note: What are some of the non-average events that come to mind in the context of digitalization? Well, one would be a customer's order being lost while being charged, this could be a rise in the price of gasoline, or this could be a banning of a popular "netizen", or this could be an event in a real, analog, world, that elicit the ripples across the digital domain.

Of course, none of the predicaments do have to happen…But, if the real-world, analog reality is to be taken, or transferred, into the digital realm, then it seems to be wise to foresee what may transpire during the process. After all, if you have your photos in your album, then the situation is different if you decided to digitize them and place them within a digital domain – somewhere in the Cloud. Consider some of the "what ifs":

1. What if someone in the picture does not want to be in the picture?
2. What if someone in the picture does not mind being in the picture, but does not like the way s/he looks in the picture?
3. What is someone who knew, or is related to, one of the people in the picture does not want that person to be in the picture?
4. And so on…

Consequently, we propose the following Implication 1:

The process of a transformation of digitalization that aims to result in a qualitatively new form of a system should start from identifying the unique characteristics of the system, and then proceed by means of small targeted changes, while being guided by non-average events.

Due to the importance of the context, it would appear that all *possible means of control are system-specific.*

The next implication that we develop is pertinent to the management of the behavior of a system that approaches the edge of chaos. The managing of the behavior of such system is *a process of controlled increase of the induced into the system gradual chaos.* There are three ways to control chaos, namely:

- By altering the system's parameters in order to reduce uncertainty and increase predictability
- By applying small perturbations to the chaotic system to try to cause it to organize
- By changing the relationship between the system and its environment

Consequently, we offer Implication 2:

The process of the transformation of a complex system (e.g., digitalization) that aims to result in the change of the behavior of the existing system may avoid entry into chaotic region by either:

- altering the internal parameters of the system, or
- altering system's relationships with the environment, or
- applying small perturbations to the system.

The developed insights and implications to the process of management of the transformation of digitalization are important. According to Implication 1, *we cannot adequately prepare in advance to control the conflict environment during the process of socio-technical transformation once it becomes chaotic.* However, could we control the behavior of a system that approaches the edge of chaos or emerges from the chaotic region?

Let us consider a way of controlling chaos through the application of small perturbations (i.e., altering information flows, changing the structure of the requirements for what an acceptable post is, etc.). The important point is that by applying small perturbations to the system we *hope* that small changes in some of the system's parameters could trigger the consequent series of changes affecting the system's organization. Therefore, it is rather an indirect way of controlling the socio-technical environment.

What about the way of controlling chaos by means of changing the relationship between the system and the environment? This requires continuous tracking of the relationship between critical conditions in the environment and key parameters of digitalization, followed by the adjustment of the system's parameters in a continuous feedback process. This is also problematic, because it will require the scope of the process of transformation to expand and include critical conditions of the environment. Meaning, digitalization would have to attempt to, if not control, then to be in sync, with its external environment. And this is not easy (albeit, regularly attempted) to do without alienating the groups it needs to survive, because neither digital consumers, not digital activists want to be "in sync" on "synced" with any system they use. Consequently, and realistically considering the available options, we suggest that the complexity of the process of transformation can be controlled by means of altering the internal parameters of the system – let us take a look at what might constitute such a change in the context of digitalization.

Digitalization, as a system, rests on a socio-technical environment which we refer to as *enterprise* – a complex organization. The concept of an organization as an instance of a complex system is deeply rooted in the organizational theory and is well-established. Research in the area of complex systems produced multiple important insights, such as that complex systems tend to exhibit a pattern of *self-organization* causing the system to evolve within its environment toward order. Self-organization can be defined as *a process of spontaneous creation of complex structure(s) that emerges due to the dynamics of the complex system.*

Self-organization is not a guided, but an *endemic* response of a complex system to the constraints imposed by its environment, which takes place naturally and automatically with the purpose of increasing the level of fitness of the system (e.g., its efficiency and effectiveness). Modern enterprises and organizations exist within hypercompetitive environments, where the speed of self-organization becomes a strategic issue of being able to advance faster than competitors do. In the case of digitalization, any development and growth of the system must coincide with the increase in the *fitness* of the system. Otherwise, the increased complexity of the structure and behavior will tear the system into pieces.

Originally, the concept of *fitness landscapes* was introduced in biology and referred to an idea of *mapping a structure of the system to its level of fitness.* Later, the concept of *ruggedness* was introduced to characterize a fitness landscape, where it was reflected by the product (e.g., N^*M) of the *number of the components* of the system (e.g., N) and the *number of interconnections* between the components (e.g., M). One of the important points of note is that an increase in the number of components gives rise to *rugged landscapes* – those are landscapes containing multiple fitness peaks and valleys. Unfortunately, an increase in ruggedness of a landscape via creation of peaks and valleys prevents the system from *ever adapting to its optimal level*. Such detrimental result of the increase in the number of system's interconnections results in a system being caught in multiple suboptimal fitness peaks – this is often referred to as a *complexity catastrophe*.

A logical conclusion is that an optimal evolution or a transformation of a complex system takes place between the *edge of complexity catastrophe* and the *edge of chaos*. In other words, if digitalization is to develop and grow successfully, then the *system must be complex enough to evolve, but not too complex to be uncontrollable*. Resultantly, systems that are too stable or too chaotic to adapt seem to be the most vulnerable. This implies that in order to evolve and survive, the system of digitalization must be adaptive enough to allow for presence of conflicts, but not too adaptable to allow for occurrence of those conflicts that could not be resolved due to the lack of control.

Note: If an on-line retailer, or a social network, is expanding, then what is the "bridge too far"? What are the, so to speak, "natural limits to growth" for such systems? And there are such limits – not every e-commerce vendor is successful independently of the context, and no social network is "all-inclusive" as practice demonstrates.

The concept of fitness landscapes is applicable to the context of social and socio-technical organizations, and it was suggested that because the process of self-organization is context-dependent, the dynamics of the process could be influenced through the manipulation of the context. This approach relies on the varying of the density of the interdependencies of the system's components that affect the degree of ruggedness of the system's fitness landscape. This, in turn, gives rise to a variety of different patterns of the behavior of the system.

It turned out that the settings with low interdependencies produce structure-to-fitness mappings with the main features of *single-peak landscapes*, which are indicative of highly predictable dynamics of each individual component of the system. Such low-interdependence systems generate settings where local actions promote global improvement of the system, and even a step in wrong direction may result only a minor degradation of global performance. Such type of landscape design is called *robust* and is of interest to the systems that pursue policies of continuous improvement and development.

On the other hand, an increase in interdependencies between the system's components eventually results in the rugged, multi-peaked landscapes. While this automatically brings along the problem of coordination, it also promotes search and exploration that are necessary during the search for novel solutions, innovations, and new service or product development. This is relevant to digitalization, because by manipulating social distances between, for example, the activists, the system can tune its interdependencies to impact the ruggedness of its fitness landscape.

In modern enterprises (e.g., such as those supporting digitalization), *Information Systems* provide the means – *information channels* – by which multiple organizational components communicate with each other. The implication is that an information system becomes the medium that controls the density of interrelationships between the components of an organization that undergoes the process of transformation. Naturally, the implication is that:

- an increase in the number of interdependencies would contribute to the increase in complexity of organizational transformation, while
- a decrease in the number of interdependencies would contribute to the reduction of complexity.

It is easy to see that communication channels provided by an information system could be used to influence the level of fitness of digitalization and the complexity of the process of its development and transformation. For our purposes, we can define *communication channel* as an *authorized and mediated by the enterprise mediated line of communication between socio-technical components of the enterprise*. This is how, from a theoretical standpoint, we can manage a conflict environment of digitalization during the process of its development and transformation. From the perspective of the paradigm of self-organization of CST, we can introduce a term *Digital Conflict Fitness*, and offer the following definition:

> Digital Conflict Fitness refers to a structural capability of digitalization to increase or maintain its level of performance in the conflict-prone, yet conflict-controlled environment.

While determination of what constitutes a level of performance of such system as digitalization is context-dependent, enterprise conflict fitness is clearly associated with the capability to control its level of structural complexity. Meaning, if we set up an on-line retailer and a social network in Poland, and we got a similar retailer and a similar network in South

African Republic, then those could behave very differently in terms of the expectations regarding their performance (e.g., # of items ordered, # of new members, etc.), but, ultimately, their respective levels of performance would be dependent on how they manage their internal structure that supports all of the aspects of the business of digitalization.

In summary, we offer the following answer to the main question we stated in the beginning of this chapter:

Based on the insights offered by Chaos Theory and Complex Systems Theory, the behavior of digitalization during the process of its development and transformation:

- can range from order to chaos, and
- can be managed by manipulation of interdependencies between the system's components.

In the next chapter, we look at some of the ways Information Systems could be used to control the behavior of such complex system as digitalization.

READER NOTES

Main points of agreement	
Supporting arguments (why agree?)	
Main points of disagreement	
Supporting arguments (why disagree?)	
Illustrative scenarios	
Possible research problem	
Possible research questions	

22

Designing a Control System

A perspective on such socio-technical systems as digitalization or an enterprise as Complex Systems sensitive to the disturbances of the environment and characterized by periods of unstable behavior is by now well established. Furthermore, this perspective has also been extended to the context of organizational Information Systems and we present the supporting arguments in Table 22.1.

But while there is a set of insights and implications regarding the development of the functionality of the control system capable of managing the unstable behavior of organizations (see Table 22.2), there is no insights regarding the possible *design* of such system.

Assuming that the behavior of digitalization is controlled by means of a *Digitalization Control System (DCS)*, there are some valuable guidelines outlining the functionality of DCS in this regard. Namely, in order to manage the system's behavior under the threat of external and internal disturbances, DCS must establish communication channels, and then manipulate the flow of information through those channels across the system. However, at this point there are no insights regarding the possible architecture of such system; thus, it is not clear how DCS should be designed in order to generate the information required for the decision making in the first place.

Consequently, the overall goal of this chapter is to obtain a set of insights regarding a possible structural design of a DCS capable of controlling a behavior of digitalization, which we define simply as *a pattern of purposeful activities directed at the achievement of a desired state of digitalization*. In the context of this definition "desired state" may refer to "as-is" static state (e.g., state of maintenance), or it may refer to "to-be" dynamic state required for transitioning to the desired state (e.g., state of growth and development).

DOI: 10.1201/9781003304906-22

TABLE 22.1

Information System as a Complex System

Major Premise	Minor Premise	Conclusion
Complex Non-Linear Dynamic System can exhibit chaotic behavior that is studied by means of Chaos Theory	Information System is a Complex Non-Linear Dynamic System	Information System can exhibit chaotic behavior that can be studied by means of Chaos Theory
Chaos Theory can describe the general pattern of behavior of Complex Non-Linear Dynamic System	Information System is a Complex Non-Linear Dynamic System	Chaos Theory can describe the general pattern of behavior of an Information System
There are limited methods that can affect the behavior of Complex Non-Linear Dynamic System	Information System is a Complex Non-Linear Dynamic System	There are limited methods that can affect the behavior of an Information System
Complex Non-Linear Dynamic Systems are capable of self-organizing behavior that can be indirectly manipulated by means of changes in internal parameters	Information System is a Complex Non-Linear Dynamic System	Behavior of an Information System can be indirectly manipulated by means of changes in internal parameters
Complex Non-Linear Dynamic System can exhibit chaotic and self-organizing behavior, complexity of which can be indirectly manipulated by the changes in internal parameters of the system	Information System is a Complex Non-Linear Dynamic System	Information System can exhibit chaotic and self-organizing behavior, complexity of which can be indirectly manipulated by the changes in internal parameters of the system

We rely on the assumption of relativity of a goal (e.g., outcome) of digitalization, which we expect to vary depending on the context, and we focus on the systems that consider the states of their internal and external environment in formulation of their strategies. Especially, we concentrate on the context where the achievement of the system's goal is dependent on the level of performance of the system, commonly measured in terms of the levels of the efficiency of utilization of inputs (e.g., analog data), effectiveness of the production of outputs (e.g., digital data), and efficiency of conversion of inputs into outputs (e.g., all the activities involved into A2D transformation). Resultantly, we limit the scope of our inquiry to *productivity-driven systems of digitalization*.

Digitalization is productivity-driven because *it is a system based on delivery of value to its customers*, and, as a result, even in the absence of direct

TABLE 22.2

Functionality of a Control System

Goal	Requirements	Implications for Development
Management of the behavior of a chaotic system	• Understanding of non-linearity, • Appreciation of the sensitivity of the system to its *Initial Conditions*, • Understanding of a non-average behavior as a source of change	• The process of development that aims to result in a qualitatively new form of Information System should start from identifying the system's unique characteristics, then proceed by means of small targeted changes, while being guided by non-average events. • The process of development that aims to result in the change of the behavior of existing Information System could prevent entry of the system into chaotic region by either altering the internal parameters of the system, or by altering system's relationships with the environment, or by applying small perturbations to the system.
Control of chaos	• Alteration of the system's parameters in order to reduce uncertainty and increase predictability, • Application of small perturbations to the chaotic system to try to cause it to organize, • Change of the relationship between the system and its environment	• Controlling the complexity of the process of development by means of application of small perturbations or by changing the relationship between the system and its environment is problematic. • The complexity of the process of development can be controlled by means of altering the internal parameters of the system.

competition from another system, a system of digitalization would aim to minimize expenditure of the resources spent in order to deliver the value. And this quest for increasing efficiency is continuous. In a similar fashion, digitalization is effectiveness-driven. This is because, ultimately, *digitalization exists because it is capable of effectively delivering the efficiently-generated value to its customers.* And, if the customers stop perceiving what is being delivered via digitalization as value, then the customers would stop instantiating their system of digitalization.

Due to the relativity of the concepts of efficiency and effectiveness of the performance, productivity-driven systems must take into consideration performance of the competing systems. However, the dynamic nature of the open environment will cause the levels of performance of competing systems to change over time, which will require reassessment of the values of the levels of effectiveness and efficiency of the system vis-à-vis its competitors. Even in a rare situation of the absence of direct competitors a system would assess its level of performance vis-à-vis itself a month, a quarter, or a year prior.

Note: if a company A started its own digitalization initiative A', and a company B started B', then how do we decide on the relative performance of A' vis-à-vis B'? this is, of course, that A and B are not carbon copies of each other operating in the same type of the environment.

In the same way, if a social network X has been in the business for a few years now, then how do we gauge its performance against a social network Y? Especially, given the fact that they operate in their different contexts?

There is an apparent link between significant changes in productivity of the competitors of digitalization and changes in the business environment; if the level of productivity of the competitors has improved, then a productivity-driven system must respond with its own improvements in their own level of productivity.

Calls for improvements in the levels of effectiveness and efficiency are endemic to productivity-driven organizations. Significant changes in the levels of effectiveness and efficiency often require structural reorganizations (e.g., ERP, BPR, etc.) that bring about the periods of unstable behavior, which, if not managed, may escalate and become chaotic. Granted, some improvements in productivity do not require any structural transformations but simply call for a gradual type of improvements in the level of performance (e.g., TQM, BPI, etc.). However, in the absence of perfect scalability the appropriate course of action leading to improvements will change in time, primarily due to the law of diminishing returns. Resultantly, in a dynamic business environment any static model that used to describe the relationship between inputs and outputs will have a limited life span.

In the absence of an adaptive mechanism that allows for discovering the new pathways for improving overall performance of the system, a productivity-driven system of digitalization (e.g., the one based on the number of subscribers, members, or customers) will engage in the process of search and exploration, during which the number of the possible states or behaviors of that system will proliferate. While periods of search and exploration are common to dynamic complex systems, these periods also bring about the danger of a system not converging on its global maximum, and settling, instead, on multiple suboptimal local maxima. This outcome of search and exploration process will result in instability of the system's behavior and overall suboptimal performance of digitalization.

Keeping the above mentioned in mind, it is reasonable to suggest that DCS can fulfill the role of an adaptive mechanism capable of controlling the system's behavior. However, in order to do so, the design of DCS must take into consideration two questions that a control system must be able to answer, namely:

1. Relative to what context the performance of the system is going to be measured?
2. What are the determinants of the given level of the relative performance?

Let us consider a hypothetical scenario of an expanding and developing social network – in order to accommodate a large number of new members, and a large number of activists, the network must change structurally (both physically and logically) – additional servers, additional bandwidth, accounts, groups, and so on. We know now that in the case of an increased volatility of a socio-political climate of the context the network's behavior may become chaotic, thus, it must be managed. But, the key question is:

> What sort of a management system could it be and what functionality must such system possess?

We express the goal of this chapter by asking the following question: *What constitutes robustness of the design of a DCS capable of controlling the behavior of digitalization?* For the purposes of clarity, we provide the following definitions.

First, we define *robust design* of a DCS as *a design allowing for managing the unstable behavior of digitalization.*

Second, we define an *unstable behavior* of digitalization as *a behavior that is characterized by the perception of the loss of control over the process of maintaining the system's goal (e.g., delivery of value) caused by the precipitous increase in the number of the possible states or behaviors of the system.* Such situation may take place when due to the changes in the external environment, the customers change their perception of what, exactly, "the value" provided by digitalization is. In such case, the system of digitalization would begin searching for what the possible "new value" could be by means of generating a set of possible alternatives, a set of "new values", hoping that one of them hits the mark with the customers. Needless to say, every option from the set would be supported by its own structure.

The *management of a behavior* is defined as *a capability to control the number of the possible states or behaviors of a system*. A state or a behavior of a system, in turn, is determined by the set of *constraints*, and constraints serve the purpose of reducing the uncertainty about the system's state or behavior.

We define a constraint as *an attribute or a set of attributes that accurately represent a particular dimension of the environment in the model that the system uses in its decision-making process*. In line with this definition, we propose that an *unstable behavior is unconstrained* (e.g., the model is inaccurate), whether the *stable behavior is constrained* (e.g., the model is accurate). We note that a constrained model does not have to be complete. In the case of digitalization, a constrained behavior would be associated with the system delivering a "true" value to the customer – there is an agreement on both side what the value is, and how it is to be delivered. Or, in simpler terms, digitalization operates according to a correct model of what the value is, where the model is verified and validated by its customers.

Finally, taking the abovementioned points into consideration, we define DCS as *a medium that allows digitalization to reduce the uncertainty about its state and behavior by means of providing a set of constraints utilized in the decision-making process involved in the maintenance of the system's goal*. Resultantly, one of the functional requirements of DCS is associated with the capability of creating the constrained (read, *accurate*) model of the context that is utilized by the system.

The modern business environment is dynamic, and the assumption of instability of the internal and external environment is advantageous when designing DCS, for such assumption will make its design more robust. The meaning of a dynamic environment from the perspective of DCS is easy to decipher, for it implies the absence of a static set of constraints and relationships between constraints that are used in creating models of the context used in the decision-making process. Conversely, an embedded in the design assumption of stability, exemplified by fixed data and process models that describe constraints and the relationships between constraints, will greatly limit the capability of a DCS, for any significant disturbance could render a set of constraints and their relationships obsolete and invalidate the embedded models.

However, traditional approaches to *IS Development* (ISD) are based on functionalism, and due to their reliance on stable models functionalist approaches do not allow for a dynamic discovery of new relevant constraints and disposal of the obsolete ones. Nor functionalist approaches allow for the dynamic adaptation and evolution of their design models. Furthermore, it is commonly accepted that a non-linearity of interaction between the system's components, as well as the presence of emergent properties caused by non-linearity, are among some of the traits that characterize social and socio-technical systems, and it is those traits that are partially responsible for the complexity of the behavior of digitalization. But the traditional functionalist approaches to ISD employ reductionism to abstract away the complexity of not only the structure and behavior of a system, but also the complexity of the relationship between the system and its environment.

Let us consider an example of a social network built on the premise of functionalist methodologies. Such system would be a hierarchical in nature, with channels of communication between groups and individual activists that are defined and restricted. Such restriction of the flow of information serves a good purpose of reducing complexity, but it does not serve a good purpose of allowing people to interact. Furthermore, let us imagine that the social network is growing – the question is *how to scale such system up*? Clearly, if the system is comprised of M nodes * N interconnections, then the answer $2*M*N$ might not necessarily do the job.

Consequently, the use of the mainstream and extended functionalist methodologies in designing DCS will result in systems that are inadequate for managing the periods of unstable behavior that are endemic to such complex system as digitalization. New approaches could be of benefit to consider. We propose that *second-order cybernetics*, which emphasizes principles of autonomy, adaptation, and self-organization of complex systems, could serve as a valuable vantage point from which important insights regarding the design and structure of DCS capable of managing behavior of digitalization could be obtained. Because the advocated perspective is context-independent, we expect the results of this consideration to offer equally valuable insights regarding the design of a variety of digitalization variety of control system of digitalization.

But, first, let us consider a justification for why the principles of cybernetics could serve as a solid foundation of the structural design of DCS; we argue that cybernetics can provide a suitable foundation for the following three reasons:

- First, domain of inquiry of cybernetics includes not only artificially engineered systems, but also naturally evolving ones. Socio-technical organizations, such as enterprises, exemplify such engineered, yet evolving systems.
- Second, the subject of inquiry of cybernetics is goal-directed systems. Digitalization is a goal-directed system, survival of which is dependent on achievement of its goal – to deliver value to the actors.
- Third, the focus of cybernetics is on the use of information, models and control actions by goal-directed evolving systems. Digitalization is an example of such system, and digitalization actively uses information, models and control actions in order to counteract internal and external disturbances that may threaten stability of its goal-oriented behavior.

Based on this brief assessment of eligibility, the use of principles of cybernetics for designing control structures of digitalization is justifiable. However, despite fitting well for the purposes of our inquiry, cybernetics is not concerned with a structure of the control system, but rather with its function. For this reason, it cannot directly provide a prescriptive blueprint of what the possible design of a control system might look like. Therefore, we take a three-step indirect approach to outlining the conceptual design of DCS. First, we offer an overview of the general principles of cybernetic systems. Second, we outline, based on the identified principles, a set of functionalities that a cybernetic system must possess. Finally, we offer a mapping of the identified functionalities to the design components that could be used in the design of DCS.

Originally, *cybernetics* referred to *a field of study of the control and communication in complex systems* (e.g., animals, machines, etc.) – this came to be known as *first-order cybernetics*. According to first-order cybernetics, a system under study can be represented by its simplified model and perceived to be independent of its observer. Some cyberneticists felt that the emphasis in studying the systems must be placed on autonomy, self-organization, cognition, and the role of the observer in the modeling of a system. Later, this movement became known as *second-order cybernetics*.

Being a complement, rather the alternative to its predecessor, second-order cybernetics recognizes a system under study as an agent in its own right, actively interacting with the observer. And while in this chapter we are concerned with second-order cybernetics, its principles are by now so firmly embedded in the overall foundation of cybernetics that it is appropriate to discuss this subject by simply referring to it as *cybernetics*, without making a clear-cut differentiation between first- or second-order cybernetics. Overall, cybernetic systems are characterized by complexity, mutuality, complementarity, evolvability, constructivity, and reflexivity – these characteristics and their interpretations are summarized in Table 22.3. It is easy to see that the attributes of cybernetic systems are congruent to those of digitalization.

The fundamental principles of cybernetics are selective retention, autocatalytic growth, asymmetric transitions, blind variation, recursive systems construction, selective variety, requisite knowledge and incomplete knowledge – we summarize these principles and their interpretations in

TABLE 22.3

Characteristics of Cybernetic Systems

Characteristic	Interpretation of the Characteristic
Complexity	Cybernetic systems are complex structures, with many heterogeneous interacting components.
Mutuality	Components of the cybernetic system interact in parallel, cooperatively, and in real time, creating multiple simultaneous interactions among subsystems.
Complementarity	Complementarity, which is brought about by the complexity and mutuality, refers to the irreducibility of the level of analysis to any one dimension.
Evolvability	Cybernetic systems tend to evolve and grow in an opportunistic manner, rather than be designed and planned in an optimal manner.
Constructivity	Cybernetic systems tend to evolve and grow in size and complexity, while historically being bound to previous states.
Reflexivity	Cybernetic systems can enter into the feedback of reflexive self-application, which may result in the reflexive phenomena of self-reference, self-modeling, self-production, and self-reproduction.

TABLE 22.4

Interpretations of Principles of Cybernetic Systems

Principle	Interpretation of the Principle
Selective Retention	Stable configurations of the system are retained, while unstable ones are eliminated.
Autocatalytic Growth	The stable configurations, which facilitate the appearance of configurations similar to themselves, will become more numerous.
Asymmetric Transitions	A transition from an unstable configuration to a stable one is possible, while the transition from stable to unstable configuration is not.
Blind Variation	The variation processes cannot identify in advance which of the produced variants will turn out being selected.
Selective Variety	The larger the variety of configurations a system undergoes, the larger the probability that at least one of these configurations will be selectively retained.
Recursive Systems Construction	*BVSR* (blind-variation-and-selective-retention) processes recursively construct stable systems by the recombining the stable building blocks.
Requisite Variety	The larger the variety of actions available to a control system, the larger the variety of perturbations it is able to compensate.
Requisite Knowledge	In order to adequately compensate perturbations, a control system must "know" which action to select from the variety of available actions.
Incomplete Knowledge	The model embodied in a control system is necessarily incomplete.

Table 22.4. Our reader may note that those principles and interpretations map nicely to the case of digitalization.

Based on general principles of cybernetics and their implications, we can derive a set of implications regarding the required functionality of DCS. The set of proposed functionalities is summarized in Table 22.5.

A set of implications outlined above suggests the presence of a concept that is central to a productivity-driven system, namely, that of the *superior stable configuration*. In line with the principles of cybernetics, stability of the behavior a goal-oriented system is associated with presence of the successful stable configuration of the system. Given the goal of achieving a high level of efficiency of conversion of inputs into outputs, a superior

TABLE 22.5

Proposed Functionality of Digitalization Control Systems

Principle	Implication of the Principle in Regard to the Functionality of DCS
Selective Retention	DCS must not only be able to contribute to the development of the stable configurations of digitalization, but also to recognize them as such. For example, a successful product or service delivery process or a particularly productive organizational sub-structure must be identified (e.g., by using internal benchmarking?), and then retained within the system.
Autocatalytic Growth	DCS must promote the increase of the stable successful structures within the system; this could be done through the process of the organizational learning utilizing knowledge management systems.
Asymmetric Transitions	DCS must be able to recognize the inferior solutions in advance, possibly by means of simulation and modeling.
Blind Variation	While DCS might not be able to ensure the production of only successful configurations, it must be able to identify the obviously inferior ones. This could be done by means of using what-if analysis and scenario-building.
Selective Variety	DCS must allow for a large variety of its own possible configurations; this could mean that DCS should be characterized by a large number of independent components and be constructed using a "building block" approach.
Recursive Systems Construction	DCS must be able to construct stable systems by the recombination of the stable subsystems and elements, which suggests high cohesion and lose coupling of DCS components.
Requisite Variety	DCS must not be constructed for one specific purpose or with a predefined functionality; instead, it must constantly be in the process of growth and development.
Requisite Knowledge	DCS must be able to select from multiple available actions an appropriate response to a particular event. This may mean that DCS must have scenario-building capabilities, possibly utilizing modeling and simulations.
Incomplete Knowledge	DCS must not function in the closed environment; instead, DCS must be able to interact freely with not only its direct competitive environment, but with the global environment as well.

stable configuration in the context of a productivity-driven system may imply *a model of conversion of inputs into output (input-output model) characterized by a high level of relative efficiency*. Consequently, we put forward the following propositions:

Proposition 1: *Stability of the behavior of a productivity-driven system is dependent on the presence of the stable input-output model that delivers "true value" to the customer.*

Proposition 2: *Accomplishment of the goal of a productivity-driven system is dependent on the creation and implementation of a stable input-output model characterized by the high level of relative efficiency in delivering the value to the customer.*

Proposition 3: *In order to control such productivity-driven system as digitalization, DCS must be able to create and identify superior stable configurations, represented by the input-output models characterized by the high level of relative efficiency.*

Perhaps, it is useful to define what "true value" is – we use the following definition:

True value is a service delivered by digitalization that was verified and validated by the actor.

The overall set of possible interpretation for each of the requirements of DCS is presented in Table 22.6.

Keeping the relativity of the concept of efficiency in mind, the functionality of DCS can be presented as encompassing two subsets of functionalities: internally-oriented and externally-oriented. Externally oriented functionality of DCS is directed towards evaluating external competitive environment of a productivity-driven organization, as well as identifying the differences between the current state of the system and the states of its competitors. Internally-oriented functionality, on the other hand, is directed towards optimization of the level of productivity of the system (sometimes, *vis-à-vis* itself), as well as towards identification of the factors impacting the efficiency of the input-output process. We suggest that outlined above functionality of DCS could be implemented by means of using combination of parametric and non-parametric data analytic and data mining techniques, such as Data Envelopment Analysis (DEA), Cluster Analysis (CA), Decision Trees (DT), Neural Networks (NN), and

TABLE 22.6

Interpretation of Functionality of Digitalization Control Systems

Functionality of DCS	Interpretation
DCS must contribute to the development of the stable configurations of digitalization	Stable configurations allow for the presence of a consistent model depicting the process of conversion of inputs into outputs by an organization, in the form of an input-output structure delivering value to the customers
DCS must promote the increase in the stable successful structures within digitalization	Stable configurations promoted on the basis of the effectiveness and efficiency of conversion of inputs into outputs in such way, that every distinct consistent model is characterized by the distinct level of relative efficiency of conversion of inputs into outputs into outcomes (value)
DCS must be able to recognize the inferior solutions in advance	Inferior solutions represent stable configurations characterized by lower levels of effectiveness and efficiency of conversion of inputs into outputs, while superior solutions represent stable configurations characterized by higher levels of effectiveness and efficiency
DCS must allow for a large variety of its own possible configurations	A process of evaluation of the stability and quality of configurations is independent of the structure of input-output model representing a given stable configuration; single DCS must be able to evaluate many configurations and assess each one of them in terms of their ability to deliver value to the customers
DCS must be able to construct stable systems by the recombination of the stable subsystems and elements	A process of evaluation of the stability and quality of configurations must rely on information-rich components that could be reused in new processes
DCS must be able to select from multiple available actions an appropriate response to a particular event	A process of evaluation of the stability and quality of configurations must allow for variations in inputs, outputs, as well as the variations in the process of conversion itself; DCS must be able to identify not only the superior configurations, but also the factors that impact the quality of configurations
DCS must not function in the closed environment	Stable configurations must be regularly assessed and re-assessed relative to the internal and external environment of the system

TABLE 22.7

Possible Implementation of Functionality of Digitalization Control Systems

Functionality	System Requirement	Structural Components
Externally-Oriented	Detection of changes in the external competitive environment	Cluster Analysis
	Identification of the possible factors that resulted in changes	Combination of Cluster Analysis and Decision Trees
	Identification of the relative efficiency of the organization relative to its competitors	Data Envelopment Analysis
	Identification of the factors associated with the differences in the relative efficiencies of the competitors	Combination of Data Envelopment Analysis, Cluster Analysis, and Decision Trees
Internally-Oriented	Identification of the factors impacting the current level of the relative efficiency of the input-output process	Regression Analysis
	Identification of the most effective ways of increasing the level of efficiency of the input-output process	Combination of Data Envelopment Analysis and Neural Networks

Regression Analysis (RA). Table 22.7 provides a summary of how the above mentioned components could be utilized to implement the required functionality.

Results of our consideration suggest that a cybernetic-centered DCS must be constructed from the collection of platform and implementation-independent components, which are highly cohesive and loosely coupled. Moreover, DCS must be scalable, fluid, and be able to reconfigure itself in its response to changes taking place in the direct competitive and global environments. Furthermore, it must have scenario, model building, and simulation capabilities. Cybernetic-centered support system must have multiple feedback loops and information inputs from the global and competitive environments. While the proposed design of DCS capable of managing the system's behavior is in its conceptual form, the parts of the outlined functionality have been implemented widely by the practitioners and academics alike.

READER NOTES

Main points of agreement	
Supporting arguments (why agree?)	
Main points of disagreement	
Supporting arguments (why disagree?)	
Illustrative scenarios	
Possible research problem	
Possible research questions	

23

Cognitive Model for Theory of Digitalization

While any reasonable causal model is sufficient for creating a set of testable hypotheses, an application of cognitive conception would allow for the development of a fuller, more general, model. Let us consider an architect designing a house – in this scenario the architect must create a cognitive model of what that house is supposed to be. The architect may go through multiple cognitive models to decide which one is a better option, but, at the end of the day, a single final one must be settled on. And, we leave the reasons for considering one model being better than other models outside the scope of our consideration.

Having established a single coherent representation of the future house, the selected conceptual model of the house must be explicated in order to proceed with the project. Thus, based on that single conceptual representation, a variety of models could be instantiated. There could be many useful derivative models generated – an architectural drawing, a mockup of the house, a blueprint, an estimated budget to build the house, and so on. The main considerations for the instantiated models is that they:

1. *Do not violate laws of nature.* For example, the architect cannot decide that the house will levitate over the pond requiring no support. Or, an architect should not assume that the house shall withstand precipitations without having some sort of a roof.
2. *Represent a unique/specific aspect of the overall coherent mental representation.* Each model must be useful for one reason or another. Also, the architect should not be able to generate different models of the same type using the same perspective. For example, it is perfectly fine to be able to say "this is how the house's footprint would look

DOI: 10.1201/9781003304906-23

like if viewed from above", but it would be quite unexpected to hear something like "this is how the view from above will be on weekdays, and this is how it will be on weekends, and this is how it is going to be come Christmas".

3. *Are complementary to each other within the overall mental representation.* For example, an architectural drawing could be accompanied by a general floor plan, a blueprint of a floor plan, and so on. Meaning, each instantiated model reflects a specific slice of the overall conceptual model, where no duplicate models of the same type/perspective are needed, and where no important dimension is left without its representation.

4. *Are consistent with each other.* For example, the architect should not be able to create a model of a palatial 10-bedroom and 6-bathroom house with the internal pool in the form of an architectural drawing and to estimate the construction costs being two thousand dollars. It could be that there is nothing wrong with the models taken separately, but if taken together, they cannot be inconsistent within the "big picture" of the selected cognitive model of the house.

So, if we rely on cognitive model, then *theory is a mental representation of a functioning system* – this means that cognitive model of *Theory of Digitalization* requires us to construct a consistent mental representation of functioning digitalization. Importantly, that mental representation is a compilation of mental representations where main processes of each are assessable via computation. Meaning, considering a constructed mental representation of the system we should be able to instantiate a multitude of the "second order" models, but every instantiated model must allow us to increase our state of knowledge about the system – by using the model we should be able to generate coherent research questions, operationalize them in the form of null hypotheses, and get the hypotheses tested and the research questions answered. Consequently, an important main question is *What is the better mental representation of the causal relationships within the system?*

If we are guided by the rule of being consistent with the laws of nature, then the mental representation of digitalization is as of a system that receives input and generates value. Let us consider main rule that is consistent with the classical laws of nature and that will be used to instantiate the consequent, domain-specific and perspective-oriented models. Specifically, we rely on a still predominant mechanistic model of science supported by the laws and principles of Newtonian mechanics, where there are elements and the cause and effect's relationships between the elements.

Thus, the main rule to follow is that of *causality* – after all, the purpose of any theory is to predict what happens with *Y* if *X* takes place. It is of no use to simply state that, sometimes, *X* and *Y* go together – a simple statement of the presence of an association or a correlation is not very useful for explanatory purposes. Our model must be causal, where it does not contain uncaused effects, so there are no "black holes" and there are no "miracles". As a result, we formulate our cognitive model of digitalization as follows:

> Digitalization is a system that generates value for its context based on the received input that is provided to the system from its context as long as the system generates value.

Figure 23.1 depicts our cognitive model of digitalization.

This is, of course, a very general mental model. But, it must be so because its goal is to allow for generating multiple, more specific, and perspective-dependent, representations. So far, the only thing that we demanded from our model is to adhere to causality – that things do not appear from nowhere, and the things do not disappear into nowhere.

This is a model of a *healthy system* – the one that solves a problem of the following type and in the following way:

Problem: We need value.
Way of solving the problem: If we have digitalization and its input, then we will have value.
Solution: We need digitalization.

FIGURE 23.1
Cognitive model of digitalization.

Or, if expressed using rules of hypothetico-deductive logic, then:

Major premise: Digitalization generates value
Minor premise: We need value
Conclusion: We need digitalization.

Now, such constructs as "value" and "input" are, of course, necessarily very general and they must be specified and operationalized for each of the instantiated domain-specific models.

But, if this is a cognitive model of a healthy system, then we must be able to create a model that accounts for the model that is "ill" – in the sense of being *not healthy*. After all, it cannot be guaranteed that digitalization will always work in all contexts. This implies that our cognitive model of digitalization must also allow for accounting a state when the system does not generate value. In short, we must take, explicitly, the presence of the negative factors in consideration of a cognitive model. In such case, "illness" of the system could be attributed to two, likely interdependent, factors – let us start by considering them separately.

Let us contemplate the first reason for why any system may not function as intended or as expected. This reason is *internal to the system*, and let us call it "internal shock". Meaning, given the conducive environment that provides inputs to the system and values the output that the system produces, the system (e.g., digitalization) could still fail. The examples of such internal shocks, let us say, in the case of a business, are many – it could be a departure or a death of a key person, it could be a "black swan"-kind of event like an inside job directed at harming the system, this could be anything that allows us to point a finger of blame, fairly and squarely, at the internals of the system itself. Some sort of a genetic mutation that kills a biological system is a good example of an internal shock – even if the context is favorable, some systems cease to exist due to such causes.

The second reason is *external to the system*, and we will refer to it as "system shock". This is an impact on the system that is initiated by and comes from its environment. Even if the system is healthy, it may not be strong enough to survive. Again, the examples are plentiful in domains of business, biology, zoology, medicine, and so on. Changes in the business environment, appearance of a breakthrough technologies, ecological change, economic crises and wars – all those are instances of a system shock.

While some of the "internal shock" reasons are, indeed, strictly internal, the great majority of them are interrelated with "system shock" factors. For example, a departure of a key domain expert, a malicious inside job, and so on are, likely, the factors that are linked to the context. After all, an expert would not leave if there is nowhere to go, and an inside job is likely done because the "inside the system" is not as "good" as "outside the system". This allows to formulate a simple description of the *success* of digitalization, as follows:

Digitalization's ability to generate value for its context is dependent on its ability to:

- *receive inputs,*
- *withstand system shocks,*
- *convert inputs into outputs,*
- *translate the outputs into to the value.*

As a result of those considerations, we present a more complete cognitive model of digitalization in Figure 23.2. It is important to note that we are concerned with creating a cognitive model of digitalization, and not with the model of the context of digitalization. Thus, all the specifics and peculiarities of all possible contexts are outside the scope of our consideration. This is similar to a situation where an architect creates a cognitive model of a "good house" – and it is different than creating a cognitive model of a "good environment for a house".

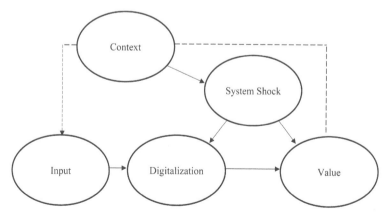

FIGURE 23.2
Expanded Cognitive model.

Consequently, the context is modeled within this cognitive model as "system shock" – all systems shocks are caused by the context, and all we know about the context we know via the generated by the context system shocks.

Let us consider a utility of the developed cognitive model of digitalization for explanatory purposes.

First, *the model is parsimonious*, because it relies on only five necessary and sufficient constructs.

Second, the model is causal, because every construct is caused by, or causes, another construct.

Third, *the model is open*, because the construct "Context" and its manifestation "System Shock" allows for accommodating whatever changes may come the way of digitalization.

Finally, *the model is easily extendible* to a variety of domains – we could approach it as being a purely technical system, or a social system, or an economic system, or a socio-technical system. We also could explore cultural aspects of the system or power relationships within it, we can view this model through the lens of social oppression or liberation.

Let us consider some of the popular frameworks that could be supported by the developed in this chapter meta-model:

1. *Resource-based view* allows approaching the construct "Value" as an important resource that digitalization generates, thus obtaining an important competitive advantage. Under this view the system of digitalization is viable as long as it is capable of generating a unique resource – the transformation of inputs into the value that is consumed by the context.

2. *Dynamic Capabilities model* yields an understanding of digitalization as of a system that can adapt to changing requirements of the context, where it is not the *value per se*, generated by digitalization at a given point in time, that is of importance. Instead, it is the capability of digitalization to change – to reconfigure itself structurally and behaviorally – as a response to the dynamic changes of the context that is of true value and interest.

3. *Transaction cost theory* gives us an opportunity to use our cognitive model as a vehicle of exploration for how digitalization gains its viability and a competitive advantage through the process of lowering the cost of transactions. The construct "Value", in this case, is a

representation of the impact delivered by digitalization in the form of more efficient transactions.

4. *Platform model* allows for viewing an impact generated by digitalization as a result of reconfiguring existing and creating new digital platforms as a response to the demands of the context. From this perspective, the construct "Value" could be represented as instance of a customized (yet standardized) digital platform supported by a smoothly integrated infrastructure (e.g., back-end-to-middleware-to-front-end).

5. *Transition theory* gives an investigator an opportunity to view the impact of digitalization as of a contributor to the process of structural and behavioral transformation relevant to transitioning from a less sustainable socio-economic system to a more "user-friendly" system. Under this take on digitalization, the "Value" could be expressed in the form of the improvements that could contribute to the process of transitioning to a better system – such as generation of new information channels and pathways, and the corresponding improvements in a socio-economic system of a given context.

6. Finally, *the theory of entrepreneurship* allows us to view digitalization as a technology-based tool allowing for generating value that is based on a recognition of new opportunities with the consequent creation of (possibly) disruptive models. This perspective allows an investigator to use the developed cognitive model to theorize, or to explain the presence of, new disruptive actors within the context of interest.

To conclude this chapter, we suggest that important questions for our reader to raise, and, subsequently, to answer, are:

1. *What in this model does not make sense?*
2. *Is there anything extraneous in this model?*
3. *Is there anything missing in this model?*
4. *How could this model be improved?*
5. *What better model could replace the proposed model?*

And, we are confident, that the set of generated answers could help our reader to better frame her own study of digitalization. In the next chapter we develop a possible version of *Theory of Digitalization* by using a cognitive model developed here.

READER NOTES

Main points of agreement	
Supporting arguments (why agree?)	
Main points of disagreement	
Supporting arguments (why disagree?)	
Illustrative scenarios	
Possible research problem	
Possible research questions	

24

Designing a Theory of Digitalization

After all the considerations of what digitalization is, what it does, and what its impact is, it is time for us to consider a more specific mechanism of the impact. One of the ways to do so is by constructing a general framework of the representation and the impact – we refer to it as *Theory of Digitalization*. Any general explanatory model relies on pre-suppositions that provide ontological and epistemological foundation of what the subject is and how it works. Thus, let us consider a set of basic assumptions that we could rely on in this endeavor of theory building:

- The perspective on digitalization is that of *systems* – we consider digitalization to be an open dynamic system.
- We consider digitalization to be a system residing within a larger dynamic system – its context.
- Digitalization and its context are socio-technical systems.
- Digitalization is instantiated by a customer residing within the context of the system, but who becomes a part of digitalization once the customer value is (potentially) identified – this is similar to a passenger instantiating a taxi cab ride to a destination.
- Digitalization receives inputs from its context.
- Digitalization transforms inputs into outputs, where outputs delivered into its context.
- The customer, and the context of digitalization, translate/transform outputs of digitalization into value.
- Generated value is what sustains the viability of digitalization within its context.
- The context of digitalization is a dynamic system and the representation of "value" changes over time – this is similar to a passenger using Uber instead of a taxi cab, or instead of using her own vehicle.

DOI: 10.1201/9781003304906-24

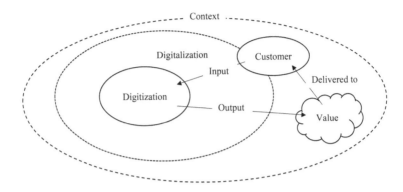

FIGURE 24.1
A basic model of digitalization for theory development.

This allows us to depict a basic model (see Figure 24.1) on which we construct our candidate theory.

For all intents and purposes, we can also express it as a set of *two states* of a Customer, where

$$State1(Customer) < State2(Customer + Value),$$

where *Value* is a benefit generated by digitalization.

The model depicted in Figure 24.1 is a loop-based model, and it is not very useful for the purposes of constructing a predictive/explanatory theory.

Thus, we can break the loop by depicting the interaction in a linear fashion.

Figure 24.2 depicts the general model of digitalization in its context, which could be further simplified as the following model represented by Figure 24.3. The model is deterministic in nature, for we know that *Input* is causal to *Digitalization*, for in order to instantiate the system (*effect*) an input is required (*cause*). We also know that *Digitalization* will produce *Output*, and *Output* will be an effect that is caused by the instantiated

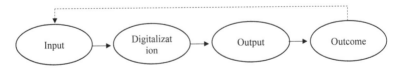

FIGURE 24.2
A linear model of digitalization for theory development.

FIGURE 24.3
A simplified model of digitalization for theory development.

system. Finally, *Output* of digitalization is going to be evaluated by the customer/context and appraised as *Impact*, where *Impact* cannot take place unless *Digitalization* produced *Output*.

However, while determinism implies causality, it does not equate with *predictability*. Thus, we cannot predict whether an input would, indeed, result in the output, and, in turn, in the intended outcome. Simply put, by doubling the input we cannot predict whether the output will be also doubled and this will result in doubled outcome (or, value) for the customer.

Consequently, at this very high level of a perspective we could offer the following proposition that is consistent with the previously developed cognitive model:

> If digitalization receives an input from its context, then it will generate an impact on its context.

It is worth noting that "impact" does not mean "significant impact" or "positive impact" – it simply means that the system of digitalization will transform an input into an output and the output will be evaluated as an outcome by its context. This is similar to an object of art – a painting – being fed into a shredder – there will be an inevitable output, albeit the value of which could be less than that of an input.

It is important to note that because digitalization is not a "black hole" that consumes inputs without a trace, and it is not a "miracle" that produces outputs out of nothing, we must consider a condition of viability of digitalization. For all intents and purposes, the "impact" must be worth producing. Meaning:

$$\$(Impact) > (\$(Input) + \$(Digitization) + \$(Digitalization'\ Transactions)).$$

It is worth noting that the "$" in the equation above does not have to be expressed in terms of a monetary value. Instead, any measurement or representation that suits the researcher's needs and interests and could be successfully defended before reviewers may do.

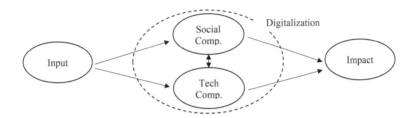

FIGURE 24.4
A model of digitalization as complex system for theory development.

However, digitalization is a complex system, and we represent it as such in Figure 24.4.

It is worth reiterating that the constructs "social component" and "technical component" comprising digitalization are logical in nature – they could be represented and operationalized via multiple physical components.

Digitalization is not a single system residing within its context – instead, there are other systems as well. Some such systems are complementary and they coexist in the state of *positive synergy* with digitalization. Other systems, however, are complementary in the sense that they coexist in *negative synergy* with digitalization. As an example, let us consider a software development company (a socio-technical system) and its interaction with the system of local education and the system of local regulation. It is fair to say that the local presence of a good system of education is a plus for a high-tech firm, so we could consider the two systems being complementary and coexisting in the state of positive synergy. A strong local regulatory system, however, may be restrictive to the business of a software development, and if this is so, then we can say that the two systems are not complementary and coexist in the state of a negative synergy.

Hence, we should expand our model to include such synergetic system. Additionally, it is useful to consider a more complex type of a complementary system, then a unidimensional one – we consider a complementary system to be a socio-technical system as well. This gives a researcher an opportunity to consider either both factors (e.g., social *and* technical) impacting digitalization, or a single one (e.g., social *or* technical). Furthermore, it allows for an opportunity to inquire into a variety of the complementary relationships – for example, an investigator could study the impact of the improved technical infrastructure of the local system of education on the social component on the software development company. Or, considering another example, this model also allows for identifying possible complementarity between investments in social capital

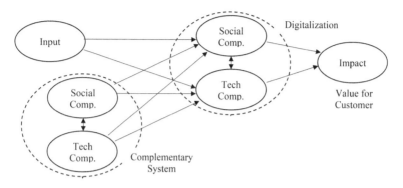

FIGURE 24.5
A candidate framework for theory of digitalization.

of digitalization and investments in social capital of the complementary system. The resultant framework is presented in Figure 24.5.

Moreover, the model could be extended in such way that "Impact" could also be represented as a collection of a social component and a technical component. This could be useful in the case of vendors of digitalization.

Let us consider a formulation of a *Theory of Digitalization* based on Figure 24.5. First, we can state that the theory can be expressed in the form of the following statements:

1. *Given a valid input, a system of digitalization will generate its impact in the form of a value for its customer.*
2. *There is a positive relationship between the levels of effectiveness and efficiency of digitalization and the generated impact.*
3. *The presence of a complementary system impacts digitalization in such way that the value for a customer is generated:*
   - *More efficiently and effectively in the case of a positive synergy.*
   - *Less efficiently and effectively in the case of a negative synergy between digitalization and a complementary system.*

For all intents and purposes, we can restate this in a very simple way, as follows:

Generation of the value by digitalization is impacted by the validity of inputs, effectiveness and efficiency of the system, and presence of complementarities.

Let us note that we did not define what a "valid" input is and whether the "value" would be positive or negative. Those are context-specific points and a decision regarding operationalizing the constructs of "valid input" and "value" must be made with the researcher's boots planted solidly on the ground in the context of a given setting.

Let us consider a small sub-set of testable hypotheses that the model above allows for generating and testing:

H01: *An increase in a quality of inputs to digitalization will result in an increase of the value generated for the customer*

H02: *An increased level of efficiency of digitalization will result in the great level of customer value generated by digitalization*

H03: *An increased quality of the structure of digitalization will result in the increased level of value generation*

H04: *An increase in the level of performance of a complementary system will result in the increased level of the performance of digitalization.*

Overall, the generated model allows an investigator for generating 10 research questions and for the consequent testing of 10 null hypotheses, as it is presented in Figure 24.6.

It is important to note that the hypotheses do not necessarily only allow for testing for causal relationships, such as where "increase in the quality of the social component of the complementary system will result in the increase in the quality of the social component of digitalization". Instead, the model allows for testing for the presence of associations. For example, based on the represented model, an investigator

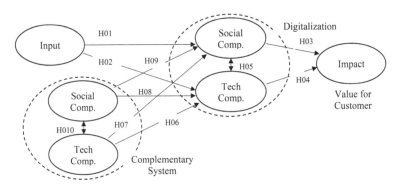

FIGURE 24.6
A possible set of null hypotheses.

may want to assess whether an increase in the quality of the inputs and an increase in the quality (e.g., possibly via such proxies as efficiency and effectiveness) of the technical component of the complementary system are associated with changes in the level of the impact produced by digitalization.

Finally, if we want to incorporate into the developed theory the construct "System Shock" that we identified as relevant in the previous chapter, then all we need to do is to incorporate it within the model above. Again, it is only expected that "System Shock" could be a social-type of a shock, or a technical-type of a shock, or it could be both. Thus, we'll represent its internal structure in the same way as we represented constructs "Digitalization" and "Complementary System". The resultant model is depicted in Figure 24.7.

We consider that the presented model is sufficiently complete to investigate the structure, behavior, and changes in the level of performance of digitalization over time. However, we suggest that our reader take those elements from the model that are useful for her purposes, and leaving those that are less useful aside. Furthermore, the resultant *Theory of Digitalization* is easy to extend by adding constructs of interest that could be introduced dependent on a given context.

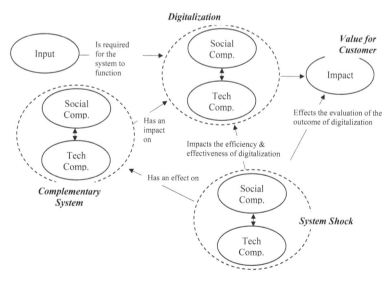

FIGURE 24.7
Proposed theory of digitalization.

Moreover, let us consider how the model could be used to ask a different sort of questions that we suggested earlier. For example, we can formulate such research questions as:

1. *How changes in perceived value of digitalization impact the socio-technical structure of digitalization?*
2. *What is the impact of digitalization on its complementary system?*
3. *What is the role of digitalization in generating system shocks?*
4. *Is there a relationship between system shocks and inputs of digitalization?*

The offered content is necessarily incomplete – the purpose of the development of the model, in step-by-step fashion, was to invite our reader to consider all the points of agreement and disagreement s/he may have, and to elicit the arguments that substantiate the points. In this way, a researcher interested in investigating different aspects and peculiarities of digitalization would not have to start from the very beginning, but, hopefully, can beneficially utilize the content developed in the chapters of this book.

READER NOTES

Main points of agreement	
Supporting arguments (why agree?)	
Main points of disagreement	
Supporting arguments (why disagree?)	
Illustrative scenarios	
Possible research problem	
Possible research questions	

Conclusion

The journey through the content of this book came to an end, and this is a good thing, for better or worse. In the worst case scenario our reader closed the text after reading a few paragraphs, and promised never to consider reading anything published by the author. In the best case the reader made plenty of notes of agreement and disagreement regarding points made in the book, only to formulate his or her own perspectives on the subject and takes on the matter. And, of course, there are scenario reflecting the points in between, where some arguments and premises were considered valid and useful, while other ones were dismissed without any consideration.

The purpose of this text was to provide any person interested in digitalization, be it a researcher or a practitioner (or any interested person, for that matter), with an opportunity to formulate their own perspective on the subject of digitalization. The arguments and propositions presented in this book, while justified, do not have to be considered correct or incorrect. Instead, they are and they should be considered as a "work in progress" stepping stones and, therefore, incomplete and unfinished. This is a very large topic, and there is an effort to be continued, if so desired, by our readers.

Similarly, one does not have to completely agree or disagree with the premises and ideas expressed in this text. Instead, our goal was to be a partner to our readers in generating original thoughts and ideas on the subject. Based on our own experience, it is often difficult to bounce ideas and exchange thoughts and perspectives, and solicit opinions on a topic of interest. This is because the field of research and practice is wide, and it could be difficult to encounter a person, close by, who is interested in the same subject. So, this book is intended to be a substitute for "such person" to anyone who is interested in digitalization. We look forward to the content of the book being critically evaluated by our readers, and we look forward to learning, from our readers, new thoughts and ideas on the subject of digitalization.

In order to build a foundation for our conceptual journey, we selected *Complex Systems Theory* and *Chaos Theory* to be our main blocks of support. While we offered a justification why those theories are suitable and

DOI: 10.1201/9781003304906-25

beneficial to use, we encourage our reader to carefully analyze the presented arguments, and, if those found deficient, to critique them and to propose better suitable alternatives. We suggested that principles of *cybernetics* could guide the development of the control system that would allow for managing the unstable behavior of digitalization. Given a relatively moderate success rate of Information Systems' initiatives and projects, it is important to formulate a well-reasoned argument for why an Information System should be build, and how, exactly, it is expected to function and for what purpose. Again, we encourage our reader to develop her own ideas on the subject and to look at the other available options and principles according to which digitalization could be managed.

Our presentation of the context of digitalization being comprised, primarily, of *digital consumers* and *digital activists* is general. We expect our readers to critique our classification and to contribute additional categories of actors instantiating digitalization. Outlined scenarios of the interactions of digital activists should be critically assessed and we hope our readers would identify those that should be replaced by the better suited ones. We look forward to learning about the new, and better suited, scenarios developed by the readers and we hope to see the results of applying those scenarios to practice or being published in academic papers.

We attempted to identify a suitable model for developing *Theory of Digitalization*. Based on the analysis of alternatives, *cognitive model* was selected. Hopefully, our reader would be able to demonstrate that better options are available and we can learn about them in upcoming publications. A structured and coherent inquiry should be based on a theory that suits the context and the topic of the study. Currently, there is no such theory in the case of digitalization – thus, we attempted to develop our own. We are looking forward to a critique of the proposed theory, and we are looking forward seeing its replacements or updates. Or, it would be interesting to actually see the proposed theory applied to an inquiry.

As we promised at the beginning of the book, this text does not contain any citations or references – this is to ease the burden of "existing studies" and to encourage our reader to apply his or her own critical analysis to the content of the book. However, we are sure that enough supporting references could be located, if needed, by using a simple keyword/phrase Web search.

Index